EISENHOWER

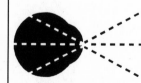

This Large Print Book carries the
Seal of Approval of N.A.V.H.

EISENHOWER

A LIFE

PAUL JOHNSON

THORNDIKE PRESS

A part of Gale, Cengage Learning

GALE
CENGAGE Learning·

Farmington Hills, Mich • San Francisco • New York • Waterville, Maine
Meriden, Conn • Mason, Ohio • Chicago

GALE
CENGAGE Learning®

LIBRARY OF CONGRESS CATALOGING-IN-PUBLICATION DATA

Johnson, Paul, 1928–
    Eisenhower : a life / by Paul Johnson. — Large print edition.
        pages cm. — (Thorndike Press large print biography)
        Includes bibliographical references.
        ISBN 978-1-4104-7794-1 (hardcover) — ISBN 1-4104-7794-0 (hardcover)
        1. Eisenhower, Dwight D. (Dwight David), 1890–1969. 2. Presidents—
    United States—Biography. 3. Generals—United States—Biography. 4. Large
    type books. I. Title.
    E836.J63 2015
    973.921092—dc23
    [B]   2014046569

Published in 2015 by arrangement with Viking, a member of Penguin
Group (USA), a Penguin Random House Company

Printed in Mexico
1 2 3 4 5 6 7 19 18 17 16 15

CONTENTS

■ ■ ■ ■

PART ONE:
EVOLUTION OF
THE PERFECT
STAFF OFFICER

■ ■ ■ ■

Dwight David Eisenhower was born on October 14, 1890, the third son, out of a total of seven sons, of David Jacob Eisenhower and Ida Elizabeth Stover. His place of birth was Denison, Texas, but when he was one, his family moved to Abilene, Kansas. This is the place where he grew up and went to school, where he is buried and where all his documents are stored in the splendid Eisenhower Presidential Library.

The Eisenhowers, who were of German origin (the name means "iron hewer"), had come to what is now the United States in 1741. They were Mennonites, an Anabaptist sect that fled European militarism and practiced the austere virtues of primitive Christianity. The father, David, received 160 acres and $2,000 from his family, but lost it all when his business failed, an event that had a powerful impact on all his boys. He was deeply religious and read the Bible in Greek, but he ruled with a stick. When Ike, as he was always known, was asked at a press conference in July 1954 about his pacifist background, he replied, laughing, "There was nothing pacific about my father." His mother, on the other hand, who played the piano and taught the boys hymns, was a passionate pacifist who wept when Ike went away to West Point, though she accepted it as God's will. His brother Milton recalled: "I never saw my mother cry until Ike became a cadet."

Ike's father worked at an Abilene creamery on Mennonite land. The family read the Bible, morning and evening, on their knees. But Ike, as an adult, never belonged to a church until he became president, when he was baptized at the Washington, D.C., National Presbyterian Church, "to set an example." But his life was always conducted within highly disciplined channels.

As a boy he rose at five a.m. to lay and light the fires. Throughout his adult life his diaries record that he habitually rose at six, and on many days worked till eleven p.m. "Seven hours' sleep is plenty," he would say. Abilene was a community that encouraged personal industry. A former cow town with a colorful past, it prided itself on being self-policing, having no crime and all its males gainfully employed. Its four thousand inhabitants were Christians of European descent, most of whom voted Republican and conformed to Norman Rockwell patterns.

Ike had blue eyes, light brown hair, an infectious grin, which was his hallmark throughout his life, and a pugnacious and competitive character. He grew to nearly six feet with a weight of 170 pounds, which never varied much. He ate sensibly, drank moderately and got regular exercise. This took the form of football, at which he excelled until a knee injury forced him to switch to coaching. His coaching skills became a huge asset in his military career, and he kept fit by taking up golf, a passion that never left him, even after he achieved a hole in one (February 6, 1968). He always stressed teamwork, as coach, general and president. He was self-assured but never conceited — humility was a much-prized Mennonite virtue. He loved hunting, fishing and camping, and he organized sporting trips. The Eisenhower boys helped one another to get through college by earning money in turn. Ike's original plan was to study law at the University of Michigan, which had one of the best football teams in the country, but his friend Everett Hazlett, with whom he exchanged letters for half a century (they are published), persuaded him to get a place at the United States Military Academy at West Point, which was free. Two applicants each year were recommended by the local U.S. senator, Joseph Bristow.

The senator held an annual competitive exam for which Ike crammed. It was exactly the kind of challenge he liked, a two-day contest involving eight bright local boys. He got 99 out of 100 in grammar, 94 in algebra, 96 in arithmetic, 90 in spelling, 79 in general history, 73 in U.S. history, 77 in geometry, and 90 in geography, and with an 87.3 average, he won a place. He always liked history and, as a boy, read a great deal of Greek, Roman and American history — and remembered it. One of his presidential speechwriters, the learned Arthur Larson, known as the Republican egghead, recalled Ike correcting him when he referred to Alcibiades the Just. "No, Arthur, you mean Aristides the Just." Ike loved reading about Lincoln, and learned passages from his main speeches by heart. From military history he loved to quote Robert E. Lee's obiter dicta, especially his key saying: "Duty is the most beautiful word in the English language."

Ike worked through the full four-year course at West Point, during what he claimed was the toughest period in its history, just before the United States entered the First World War. The life was spartan, but this was nothing new. Rote learning was the rule. Ike excelled at English and was at the top in essay writing. His talent for coaching was fully exploited and he became more devoted to teamwork, which became a salient part of his philosophy of life. He found the school fascinating: Lee's room, Grant's room, the field where Custer learned to ride. His first year as a plebe, which involved much hazing by senior cadets, was redeemed by ceremony and bands, which Ike relished. As a senior himself he never hazed plebes. He hated regimentation for its own sake. His only black mark was for smoking, strictly forbidden, which meant he was 125 out of the total intake of 164 under "discipline." His overall final position was 61 out of the 164 graduates, of whom 59 eventually became brigadier generals (one star) or higher, two of them generals of the army (five stars). Ike enjoyed West Point and greatly benefited from it. His knee injury ruled out the cavalry, so his first posting, as a second lieutenant, was to the infantry at Fort Sam Houston, Texas, in 1915.

Ike developed one lifelong characteristic at West Point: a tendency to conceal any intellectual interests or cerebral accomplishments. "Academic" was a term of abuse at the Academy. He liked to be considered a "regular guy" and took to reading Westerns to hide his passion for military history. This curious practice became habitual. Richard Nixon said to me: "I served General Eisenhower as his Vice-President for eight years. He was by far the most devious man I ever met in my life."

He was also exceptionally well mannered and courteous. He was capable of ferocious bouts of temper, but these were kept under strict control and unleashed only when required for a definite purpose. All this he owed, in the first instance, to his wife, whom he married in July 1916. Mamie Geneva Doud was born in Boone, Iowa, but the family moved to Denver when Mamie was seven, and that is the place with which she identified. Her father had made a modest fortune in meatpacking, and the family was affluent. Her father employed a chauffeur, and Mamie had her own lady's maid. At sixteen she was sent to Miss Wolcott's finishing school, Denver's "prime academy for young ladies." She thought Ike "the best-looking man

I had ever met," and while determined to marry him, she was also
clear about the ways in which he
could be improved. She spotted immediately that he was a man of
unusually high intelligence with a
strikingly wide vocabulary, but she
removed many rusticities from his
manners and accent and the rough
traits he had acquired at West Point.
As she had a horror of flying, she
also forbade his half-formed notion
of becoming an army flier (he had
begun taking lessons) and got her
father to tell Ike that the marriage
could not take place unless he
renounced any such ambition (Ike
complied).

"It was a case," Mamie said, "of
someone from a family of boys

mating with someone from a family of girls — I had three sisters and no brothers." They had quite a hard time of it living on army pay. They moved more than twenty-five times in Ike's army career, and never owned a house until they bought their retirement home, a farmhouse at Gettysburg, Pennsylvania. "I learned a lesson, early," she confessed ruefully. "Our first big move, I sold the household furniture, which included some valuable wedding presents. I thought it would be simpler. All I got was $95! It took us years and years to replace them properly. So in future I never parted with anything. Put it into storage, if necessary, and filled the attic with old clothes."

Mamie was tremendously important to Ike at every stage of his life and career. They got on because each respected the other's markedly different habits. Ike never got up later than six a.m., except in very unusual circumstances. Mamie preferred, like Churchill, to do her administrative work in bed and rarely rose before ten a.m. or even noon. As they advanced up the pyramid, Mamie regarded Ike's working times and areas as sacrosanct and never penetrated them. "When Ike was President I only went into the Oval Office four times, and each time I was invited." On the other hand, she had a remarkable memory for faces and names, was a frugal housekeeper, however large the establishment, and kept everything that was within her province under tight control. J. B. West, the chief usher at the White House, said: "She had a spine of steel, formed by years of military discipline. She understood a large household, knew exactly what she wanted every moment and exactly how to get it done." She trimmed down the staff, imposed a no-talking rule and kept her own schedules strict military secrets.

Ike himself asserted, of his presidency: "She made the White House livable, comfortable, and meaningful." And: "I got it into my head I'd better listen when she talked about someone brought in close to me." And: "I always sought Mamie's advice on financial matters. She was keen on budget savings. Yes, Sir!" Mamie was never pretty, but she was always trim and did Ike credit. With a height of five feet four inches and about 135 to 140 pounds in weight, which never varied much, she was named in 1952 one of the best-dressed women in the world by the New York Dress Institute. She popularized short bangs, pastel-colored stockings and Elizabeth Arden's Main Chance health spa in Phoenix, Arizona. When Ike ran for office, rumors flew that Mamie drank. Someone had the hardihood to raise the issue at a press conference in 1953. Making a visible effort to control himself, Ike said: "To the best of my knowledge, Mrs. Eisenhower has not had a drink for eighteen months." But it was Mamie herself who finally laid the issue to rest in 1973 during a TV interview, when she said that a carotid sinus condition sometimes affected her balance. (She also suffered from a mild form of claustrophobia.) This would explain why she was sometimes said to be unsteady on her feet. Whether alcohol ever contributed to this behavior is unclear: the evidence is contradictory. She was never a chronic drunk — far from it — and my view is that the stories about her drinking were invention, circulated by political enemies of Ike's who found him an extraordinarily difficult man to attack on personal grounds.

What is indisputable is that Mamie made Ike a good and loving wife and was a distinct asset in his career, especially in its early stages. While the First World War lasted, Ike prospered mightily. From Fort Sam Houston he was sent to Fort Oglethorpe, Georgia, as an instructor in the Officers' Training Corps, and promoted to captain, then sent to Fort Leavenworth, Kansas. He then became involved in the Tank Corps, a rapidly expanding branch of the army, first at Gettysburg, then at Camp Meade, Maryland. His enthusiasm led to rapid promotion, first to major, then to lieutenant colonel. He was on notice for overseas service when the signing of the armistice in November 1918 suddenly put military expansion into reverse. Ike found himself returned to his substantive rank, captain, then promoted to major, in which he remained for sixteen years.

Moreover, his keenness for armored warfare was ill regarded by his superiors, who stigmatized it as arrogant and impertinent, especially as he was still nominally an infantryman and without battle experience of any kind. His application to attend the Command and General Staff School at Leavenworth was savagely turned down, and instead he found himself executive officer of the Twentieth Infantry Brigade in the Panama Canal Zone.

This disappointment, however, turned out to be a blessing. It brought him to the attention of General Fox Conner. This gifted and unusual man was the first of Ike's guardian angels in his career. He had been chief of staff to General John J. Pershing, was a staff officer of exceptional brilliance and recognized the same propensities in others. He could see that Ike was a born staff man with an unusual combination of qualities. Conner reported that Ike was precisely the kind of officer who ought to attend the Staff School, and saw to it that he went there in 1925. Ike loved the school and came out first when he graduated the following year.

What were the qualities Conner spotted? First was a clear, analytical intelligence. Second, he had the ability to articulate conclusions in excellent English — any kind of paperwork came naturally to him. Third, he could get on well with anyone, especially hard cases — which were common in an army where thrusting individualism was encouraged and promoted. He was, fourth, adept at resolving differences and promoting solutions, especially compromises that worked. Fifth, he had admirable persistence in pursuing reason in any military enterprise. Sixth, he concealed his strengths. Seventh,

Ike was very hardworking, often for prolonged periods, yet he always appeared relaxed. All these qualities were bound together by an eighth virtue: consistent aims in life, quietly but vigorously followed. The effect of the Staff School was to confirm this combination, and especially to enable Ike to get his thoughts onto paper in a pellucid manner, something very rare in the U.S. Army, indeed in any army. It also implanted in Ike a keen realization of the connection between military power and industrial capacity, which became a salient part of his thinking about the future.

Ike's high ratings at the Command and General Staff School should have ensured him a wide choice of military posts when he graduated. And indeed for a short time in 1926–27 he was commander of the Second Battalion of the Twenty-fourth Infantry. But he then chose to serve on the American Battle Monuments Commission, under the auspices of the Army War College. This took him to Washington, D.C., and to its Paris headquarters, for the best part of 1928 and into 1929. As Ike often complained that his one aim was to serve with battle troops, it may seem curious that he volunteered for this post. The reasons are that it involved travel, which he and Mamie enjoyed; that it brought him into contact with senior officers from all arms of the service; but above all, that it involved tricky and arduous administrative tasks of a kind he was beginning to relish, and perform well.

An examination of letters written by Ike during his service on the ABMC shows him to have become a meticulously efficient administrative officer who wrote clear, correct and pungent English, and was an inveterate enemy of muddle, jargon and bureaucracy. A characteristic remark reads: "In my opinion we cannot afford to permit years of work in obtaining accuracy as to fact to be vitiated by looseness in expression. Exactitude is the primary consideration." The post also allowed him to develop his style in dealing with tact and finesse with both superiors and subordinates. "Ike was in a job where emotions ran high," said a colleague, "but he contrived to make many friends — and no enemies." In recognition of his first-class service with the Commission, his next posting was as executive assistant to the assistant secretary of war, in Washington, D.C.

This brought him to the heart of things at the War Department, and he was there from November 1929 to February 1933. His task was industrial mobilization, his chief duty being to prepare plans for making optimum use of the nation's resources, including raw materials and manpower, in the event of a major war. He said he was "looking forward to the opportunity of learning something about the economic and industrial conditions that will probably prevail in this country in the event of major war." He also supplied staff support to the War Policies Commission, and in this body he moved close to two men who became among his warmest admirers: the future generals Leonard Townsend "Gee" Gerow ("my best friend for years") and Wade Hampton "Ham" Haislip. The latter was the great expert on budget and legislation, and laid the foundations of what became Ike's encyclopedic knowledge of how Congress worked and how to put the army's case to politicians.

Ike was involved not just in paper-work and argument but also in traveling to see to practical matters. He visited New England to frustrate attempts to shut down handgun factories (including Smith & Wesson) in response to the crime wave created by Prohibition. He also visited estates all over the United States and in Central America to study rubber plant cultivation, which proved vital in the Second World War because of the Japanese occupation of Malaya. These activities produced superb reports. More important was the War Department's "Complete Industrial Plan for War," which Ike wrote single-handedly. Previous efforts by the planning branch he dismissed as "hopeless," and he started from scratch. Coordination within the government led him to push the idea of an executive assistant to the president with cabinet rank, to handle, on behalf of the president, all War Department business and act on all defense decisions. By the end of 1930, this document of Ike's, titled "Plan for Industrial Mobilization 1930," was complete. It covered all aspects: price and trade controls, raw materials procurement, labor, utilities, transportation, coordination of executive efforts and draft legislation authorizing the creation of special agencies. It was bound in leather and sent to President Herbert Hoover, was accepted and became the basis of official policy.

Ike began to attract notice, not all of it congenial. Planning for a future conflict was denounced as "war-mongering" in the *Nation* and various local papers. Ike wrote papers rebutting such charges, and drafted speeches at the Army War College delivered by his boss, Frederick H. Payne, the assistant secretary. He wrote in his diary: "For two years I have been called 'Dictator Ike' because I believe that virtual dictatorship must (in certain conditions) be exercised by the President. I have learned to keep still — but I continue to believe it." In June 1932 he started keeping a diary. The first entries were called "Notes on Men" and profiled all the politicians and senior officers concerned with defense. It was one of the best things he ever did and survives in the files.

Plans to reward Ike's work by making him a one-star general (brigadier) ran up against insuperable difficulties. But in January 1932, General Douglas MacArthur, the army chief of staff, made him what he termed his senior aide and chief assistant. As such, he was alongside the general when, on July 28, 1932, he carried out Hoover's orders to disperse the shantytown that the so-called Bonus Marchers had set up in Washington, D.C.

No episode in American history has been the basis for more falsehood, much of it deliberate. The Communists did not play a big role in setting up the camp, but they organized the subsequent propaganda with great skill. The officer in charge of the dispersal, at the command of General MacArthur, was Major George S. Patton Jr. For once in his life he behaved with commendable restraint. Indeed, the whole operation was most delicately conducted. But there were tales of cavalry charges, of the use of tanks and poison gas, of a little boy bayoneted while trying to save his rabbit and of tents and shelters being set on fire with people trapped inside. There were published such works as W. W. Walters's *B.E.F.: The Whole Story of the Bo-*

nus Army (1933) and Jack Douglas's *Veterans on the March* (1934), both almost entirely fiction. A book of ballads of the Bonus Expeditionary Force, as the marchers called themselves, appeared, including such items as "The Hoover Diet Is Gas" and "I have seen the sabres gleaming as they lopped off veterans' ears." While the camp was burning, it was stated, Hoover and his wife, who kept the best table in White House history, dined à deux in full evening dress off a seven-course meal. Some of these fictions were still being repeated in respectable historical works even in the 1970s.

A factual and truthful account of the dispersal of the camp was meticulously put together by Major Eisenhower and widely circulated. It was signed by MacArthur as his report, but every word was written by Ike and it told a story of careful forbearance and restraint. It should have made unnecessary the subsequent investigation, marred by acrimonious disagreements between the police and the attorney general. But unfortunately, little of it was reproduced in the press. What Ike learned from this episode was the absolute necessity to keep journalists well informed and friendly, and the lesson was one he applied with outstanding success throughout his public career. With hindsight he thought that a well-prepared press conference held on the evening of the dispersal would have worked wonders with the public. He came to believe strongly in this device, and personally held more than five hundred during his career.

Needless to say, Ike's report on the veterans put MacArthur in the best possible light, and the general invited his help when, on retiring as army chief of staff, he was appointed to the Philippines to create its armed forces in preparation for self-government. The Tydings-McDuffie Act of 1934 granted the islands commonwealth status and full independence ten years after the formation of a government. MacArthur, whose substantive rank was only major general, was a military adviser, and was termed a field marshal. In addition to his army salary he was paid an extra $3,000 a month, making him the highest-paid military officer in the world. Ike, as assistant military adviser, also did well, drawing $980 a month pay, plus living allowances. Ike, needless to say, did most of the work, the general supplying "the theatrical bits," as Ike put it. It often meant a long day — six a.m. to eleven p.m. — but was valuable experience. He decided on the equipment in detail and made many trips to the United States to order it. This brought him into contact with leading armaments corporations — Winchester, Colt, Enfield, et cetera — and Ike learned how to drive hard bargains and get products, especially ammunition, at special prices. His diaries tell a fascinating story. The entry for September 25, 1938, reads: "Visit to American Armament factory at Rahway was instructive. I took Colonel Hughes, Ordnance, with me to inspect the plant. . . . All problems that have been bothering Ordnance, such as tin assembly, capsule form, fuses (deformation of point) etc. have been attacked by company and a solution found. Have asked for latest prices to compare in detail with Ordnance Dept. Spent long time here." In the buildup of Philippine forces, Ike acquired a good working knowledge of military aircraft, and he flew them himself. He took his final flying exam and passed in July 1939 with 350 hours of pilot time and 140 hours of observer time. (He later liked to boast that he was the first certified pilot to occupy the White House.) He also learned to pilot Thornycroft ships, and to buy them.

The relationship between the practical Ike and the prima donna MacArthur was always edgy. The general's comments on Ike varied according to mood: "The best officer in the Army." "The best clerk in the Army." "Just a chief clerk." Ike approved of the early New Deal and liked FDR's (Franklin Delano Roosevelt's) methods — his diary notes are particularly shrewd and perceptive. MacArthur disliked the New Deal and when Ike contradicted his view that Alf Landon would win by a landslide, he was furious. Ike disliked the way MacArthur, while Ike was away on armament trips to the United States, altered all his carefully prepared plans, often for venal reasons. His diaries list his boss's greed, his anti-FDR rants, his secret plans to run for vice president and, not least, his affair with the Scottish-Eurasian Filipina Isabel Cooper — letters to whom had eventually to be bought back for $15,000. There was an inevitable row, Ike recording: "It is almost incomprehensible that after 8 years of working for him, writing every word he publishes, keeping his secrets . . . he should suddenly turn on me, as he has all the others who have ever been around him. He'd like to occupy a throne room surrounded by experts in flattery."

However, Ike took trouble to remain on good terms with Mac-Arthur, publicly at least. He also established excellent relations with President Manuel L. Quezón, the first head of the newly formed Philippines government. He played bridge with him and allowed himself to be used, discreetly, as a counterpoise to MacArthur. Ike was never deliberately Machiavellian in his relations with important people, but it was a matter of policy for him to be friendly with key politicians and with the senior officers of all the services. He always wrote to congratulate them on promotions or appointments to significant or enviable posts. By March 1939, however, he felt that his spell in the Philippines, though valuable, had served its term. He recorded in his diary: "There is no head of this office, except the General — who is now here only an hour a day — everyone does as he pleases and no real coordinate progress is possible. I'm ready, more than ready, from a professional point of view, to go home . . . as soon as I can decently go." He finally left in December 1939, after the war in Europe had started. He wrote a detailed memo to President

Quezón, summing up all the work he had tried to do to bring the local forces up to standard and outlining what remained — a formidable piece of work much appreciated by the president, who took a generous view of Ike's claim for moving expenses. The move was a major operation, for Mamie had accumulated a great deal of what Ike called junk, including a precious piano. There was also a spool bed from Ike's old home in Abilene. This went with them everywhere, including the White House, and still exists, though now in a museum.

Ike had been promoted to substantive lieutenant colonel on July 1, 1936, and by 1940 was widely regarded as one of the most experienced staff officers in the army. He had never commanded troops, except on a temporary basis. He had never been in action. But who had? Between November 1918 and December 1941 no American army unit had been engaged in combat, and officers who had experienced war were a generation out of date. Because of the peculiar nature of his duties, Ike was at least familiar with the latest procedures of staff routine, with new armaments, aircraft and landing craft (such as they were then). He also had a very useful familiarity with government procedures and knew many politicians in Washington. He was probably better trained, all round, than any other staff officer in the army — there were not many of them anyway — and he was becoming known in military circles as reliable, skillful and easy to get on with. I state this because it was often asked, later, how it happened that an officer of the age of fifty-one when America entered the war in December 1941, who had been stuck in the rank of (substantive) major for sixteen years and had never heard a shot fired in anger — this was a point monotonously brought up against Ike, notably by his British contemporaries, and especially Field Marshal Bernard L. Montgomery — suddenly rose in rank to command millions of men. The answer is that, unconsciously, Ike had been preparing to do it for many years, and was almost certainly the best available, in general experience, for the top job he got.

In 1940, he held various staff commands until he was made chief of staff of the Third Infantry Division, based at Fort Lewis, Washington. Thence he moved to the army's IX Corps at the fort, and later was staff chief of the Third Army at San Antonio, Texas, being promoted in turn to full colonel and brigadier general (one star). These changes brought him closer to General George C. Marshall Jr., the army's chief of staff, who already knew all about Ike and already had his eye on him as a potential winner in the event of war. In this Marshall agreed with MacArthur. Though in certain moods MacArthur would dismiss Ike as "the apotheosis of mediocrity" and "a highly literate nincompoop," he was also sure that if the United States got involved in a major war, he would do exceptionally well. So was Marshall.

Marshall was fond of pointing out that although Ike had been graded by senior officers many times, the only one to give him a poor rating was Lieutenant Colonel Xenophon Price, who had served over Ike at the Monuments Commission. "But then," added Marshall, "Xen Price is an engineer, and engineers, for reasons which are a mystery, *always* give low ratings." All of Ike's other ratings had been excellent, and he was particularly commended for his ability to get on with everyone.

Of the competition there was General Patton, who cut a prominent figure as a former cavalryman, now regarded as the U.S. Army's best tank commander. Patton was a superb thruster whom Ike had known from his own abortive armored days. But he was always in rows and regarded as "defective in self-control." His chances of becoming the Guderian or the Rommel of the American army were judged to be dependent on his skill in staying out of trouble. Another rising star was Mark Clark, a first-class officer and friend, and a warm admirer of Ike's, whose all-round experience made him sure of high command in a rapidly expanding army. But he aroused suspicion because it was felt he was self-promoting. He employed a public relations officer when he was only a lieutenant colonel, and by 1941 was already well on the way to assembling a PR team which eventually totaled more than fifty (of all ranks).

Ike was also conscious of the need to devote attention and forethought to his own public relations, but he was much more discreet about it, and certainly never acquired the reputation, from which Clark suffered throughout his career, of putting PR above professional military skills. In fairness to Clark, it must be said that he lost no opportunity to promote Ike's interests as well as his own. He was tireless in bringing Ike's name before key people at the War Department, and lobbied on his behalf among the Washington press corps.

Probably the most promising one-star general at the outbreak of war was Omar Bradley, who had been Ike's contemporary at West Point and had climbed slowly up the ladder too. Bradley was classified as "sound" rather than brilliant. But this was no handicap in a peacetime army, and Marshall thought highly of him.

With the outbreak of war in Europe, and Ike's return to the United States, he and Marshall inevitably drifted closer together. I use this term because their relationship was fated. Marshall was the chief of staff, and Ike was the best staff officer in the army. Marshall's importance in American history has never been properly appreciated. He was one of the key figures of the twentieth century, and like Ike he was a major figure both in the military and in politics. Ike was never in any doubt about Marshall's qualities. His son John recorded that after the war, he was asked to name the five greatest men he had encountered in his career. He asked for time to think, and then called for a pencil and paper. He then wrote down, slowly: "General George Marshall, John Foster Dulles, Air

Chief Marshal Sir Peter Portal, General de Gaulle, and Winston Churchill." Marshall was the first name that came to his mind, and was written first. When Ike was asked a similar question five years later, he produced exactly the same list, though in a different order. But again Marshall's name came first. He was fond of saying, "The two men I have worked closely with over the years were MacArthur, for seven years, and Marshall, for four. I have reservations about both but for Marshall I have affection too. He was a really good man." There is little doubt that Ike regarded as his greatest error of judgment the occasion when, running for president in 1952, he omitted a paragraph in praise of Marshall's loyalty, on the advice of campaign "experts" who feared it would antagonize Senator Joseph McCarthy. But we will deal with that in its place. Here it is important to note that on first getting to know Marshall, Ike found him "chippy," "cold" and "austere." Famous charmers failed totally to get close. FDR tried to call him George but was rebuked: "General Marshall, if you don't mind, Mr. President." He never used the name Ike. It was always Eisenhower until November 4, 1952, when it changed to Mr. President.

Marshall's opinion that Ike had exactly the qualities needed to take a top role in the vast war that was engulfing the world was strengthened as they met and worked together. Marshall particularly hated self-seeking officers who put promotion first in their priorities; buck passers; officers who would not, or could not, delegate; officers who shouted and pounded the desk; those who loved the limelight; and the pessimists. Ike had none of these defects. On the contrary, he scored a definite plus in all these categories. He also scored high in two qualities that won Marshall's (always grudging) approval. He was offensive minded, and he always concentrated on the opportunities rather than the difficulties in any given situation. Marshall particularly valued Ike's willingness to accept responsibility. What he did not know, but would have strongly approved if he had, was that Ike took out any frustrations in his diary, a safety valve also used by Sir Alan Brooke, Marshall's equivalent in the British Army.

The American forces began to expand rapidly from September 1939, and on a gigantic scale from the middle of 1940, after the French collapse and the emergence of Germany as an absolutely dominant military power in Europe. Suddenly everything changed radically at the War Department. Luck is a vital element in any career, and Ike had always been lucky. In the crucial year 1941, when the United States was on the brink of war, his luck held. He became chief of staff to General Walter Krueger of the U.S. Third Army. This was at Krueger's request — Ike was getting known — and on the eve of what became the largest and most critical maneuvers in U.S. history, to take place in Louisiana in August and September.

The eve-of-war hysteria meant these originally routine army rehearsals attracted unusual public interest, and were enlarged in scale. Krueger's force was expanded to 240,000 men and pitted as an "invading army" against a "defensive" Second Army of 180,000 men. A large press corps, including star columnists from Washington, D.C., and New York, was assembled to provide coverage. The "invasion" was a huge success, and Colonel Ike, who had worked hard to make it so, and had scarcely gone to bed the entire fortnight the maneuvers lasted, was given the credit. In particular Drew Pearson and Robert S. Allen, who wrote a much-admired column in the *Washington Post,* brought the colonel's name to the attention of the American public in a highly congratulatory article, which was read by everyone from FDR down. It was the turning point in Ike's career. How much Ike had to do with this particular article, or the press treatment in general, is arguable. The article misspelled his name. But this may be typical obfuscating tactics, with which students of Ike's handling of the press were to become familiar. Ike said that General Krueger should have been given the credit. But then he would say that (privately), wouldn't he? The episode got Ike his first general's star, on October 3, 1941. More important, on December 12, 1941, shortly after Pearl Harbor, Ike got a phone call ordering him to report to General Marshall with all possible speed.

■ ■ ■ ■

Part Two: Learning to Command Millions

■ ■ ■ ■

Ike reported to General Marshall at the War Department on December 14, 1941. The general outlined the rapidly deteriorating situation and asked: "What should be our general line of action?" Ike replied: "Give me a few hours and I'll produce a detailed plan." That evening, using his typewriter, he produced one on yellow lined scratch paper. He seized on the importance of Australia as a forward U.S. base. He said that the

Philippines could not be saved, but the effort should be made. The rest of Asia "may excuse failure but they will not excuse abandonment." Marshall, Ike noted, had "an awfully cold eye. He said: 'Eisenhower, this Department is filled with able men who analyze their problems well but feel compelled to always bring them to me for final solution. I must have assistants who will solve their own problems and tell me later what they have done.' " Ike: "Understood." He found Marshall "the Ideal Boss," both to work for and as a teacher. He said: "I wouldn't trade one Marshall for fifty MacArthurs. My God, that would be a lovely deal! What would I do with fifty MacArthurs?"

By contrast, Ike got to hate Admiral Ernest J. King (as did all the British). He said he was "the antithesis of cooperation, a deliberately rude person . . . a mental bully. One thing that might help with this war is for someone to shoot King." Ike stood up to him and King changed his tune. Later he became one of Ike's strongest supporters. By the end of March 1942, Ike was a major general (two stars) and head of War Plans, foreseeing a five-million-man army. A dramatic tale is told by the rise of military spending as a percentage of the federal budget. In 1936 and for the two following years, it was as low as 3.9 percent. In 1939, it had risen to 11.9 percent, by which time

FDR had envisaged America's eventual entry into the war as inevitable. By 1941, it was nearly a third of the budget, 31 percent. In 1942, by which time Ike was running the War Plans Division at the War Department, it was nearly two thirds: 64 percent. By this time Ike had 107 officers working directly under his command at the Operational Plans Department, as it was now called, controlling projects all over the world.

Lucian K. Truscott Jr., who watched Ike at work at this time, recorded: "Every view was considered. Each point was carefully analyzed. Ike had an extraordinary ability to place his finger at once upon the crucial fact in any problem, or the weak point in any proposition [and] to arrive at quick and confident decisions." He added: "Whatever the pressure, he had a charming manner and infinitely good temper." Ike's emphasis was always on the team. He wrote in his diary in April 1942: "In wars such as this when high command invariably involves a president, a prime minister, six chiefs of staff, and a horde of lesser planners, there has got to be a lot of patience — no one person can be a Napoleon or a Caesar." He had a saying: "Don't curse. Give it a smile." By March 1942, Ike had grasped that in terms of major items of equipment, the overwhelming emphasis must be on aircraft carriers and self-propelled landing craft, not battleships, with which the admirals were still obsessed. This was one reason he found King hard to take. Ike was dismayed, on arriving in Washington, D.C., by the poor quality of high-level intelligence, especially of an industrial nature. All the work he had done in this field in the 1930s immediately came to the fore. Granted the overwhelming, and rapidly expanding, capacity of the U.S. industrial base, compared to Japan's, America was bound to win the Pacific war, given time and elementary common sense.

Hence, Ike wholeheartedly endorsed the top-level decision to give priority to Europe, as did

Marshall. By the end of April 1942, he had decided to send Ike there to take charge and command U.S. forces in the theater, which were now beginning to arrive in growing numbers. Ike arrived in London in May and found a deplorable "peacetime state," as he put it angrily. The American officer in charge, Major General James E. Chaney, and his staff still wore civilian clothes, worked an eight-hour day, took weekends off and had minimal contacts with the British government and high command. Ike changed all this in twenty-four hours, and called for Mark Clark, an expert in training for operations, to join him. They went to see Churchill together and impressed him: "Two splendid young American generals!" Churchill did not like long and difficult names and coined the phrase "I like Ike." Field Marshal Alan Brooke, the British chief of staff, was a problem to begin with. He had the loudest voice in the army: "Why does he have to shout at me?" asked Ike. But Brooke soon came to recognize Ike's strategic sense, his mastery of detail and his fertility of ideas, pronouncing him "a good egg." With Louis Mountbatten, the British head of Combined Operations, Ike got on well from the start. Ike admired the way he thought in terms not of army, navy and air, but of total power, while Mountbatten found Ike's optimism "refreshing" and his enthusiasm "catching."

There was an absolute need at this time to do something to take the Nazi pressure off the Russians. Until the Battle of Stalingrad, there was absolutely no guarantee Russia would survive Hitler's onslaught. A real fear of a Russian collapse was the background to Allied strategic arguments in 1942. Taking their cue from Marshall, Ike and his colleagues argued for an early assault on northwestern Europe. Churchill and Brooke thought this a certain formula for catastrophe. The Nazis had a million slave laborers erecting obstructions and blockhouses on all the likely sections of the coast — Hitler's "West Wall" —

and the Americans had yet to discover just how formidable was the German Wehrmacht, "the finest professional army in the world," as Brooke put it. Ike, at this stage, thought the Mediterranean "a sideshow" and the British obsession with it part of their imperial postwar plotting. On the other hand, it offered chances for American troops to come to grips with the Germans and gain battle experience without risking annihilation. As Churchill put it, "Here are two splendid armies building up, American and British, but not yet killing a single German, while the Russians are holding down 185 divisions."

A Mediterranean thrust, which

would give the Americans indispensable battle experience in preparation for an eventual Atlantic thrust, proved an irresistible argument, and eventually took the form of Operation Torch, an Anglo-American-Canadian series of landings in Morocco, Algeria and Tunisia, the western arms of a pincer, of which Montgomery's Eighth Army in Egypt was the eastern fang. The early stages of Torch were settled in London, to which Ike, with full powers, returned on June 24. The following day he held a highly successful press conference — his first — from which he emerged, to judge by the coverage, as a world figure, remaining one for two decades, until January 1961, when he retired as president.

Ike was more successful at public relations than any other major figure of the twentieth century. It is not going too far to suggest he had a genius for the art, more so even than FDR, and it is noteworthy that he was already fifty-one when he first spoke to members of the press as a group, the first of so many occasions. It is a remarkable fact that Ike always got the press on his side, with three exceptions: his deal with Admiral Jean François Darlan in 1942, recognizing him as commander of French forces in North Africa; his handling of Senator Joseph McCarthy (to begin with); and his civil rights policy of 1954–61. Except for these, from which he learned a great deal, Ike always had the press working for him, often very hard. His formula was simple: careful, conservative dress, uniform freshly pressed ("Ike always appeared to be wearing his uniform for the first time," said Mark Clark). Always stand erect. Square your shoulders. Hold your head high. Speak bluntly but clearly. Use homely expressions. Look the camera straight in the eye. Cameramen, both flash and TV, loved him. Hard to say which they preferred: Ike grim or grinning. Either usually got a two-column, front-page slot.

Ike's personal "family" stayed with him throughout the war. Harry Butcher, his PR man, had been a journalist, magazine editor and CBS radio official. He also had the job of keeping Ike's daily journal. His secretary was Mary Alice Jaqua, "a devil for late-night typing sessions." An Irish divorcée, Kay Summersby, was his driver and reputed lover. Ike denied this (to Mamie), but admitted she was "a peach." Mickey McKeogh looked after his comfort and well-being, and wrote regularly to Mamie about Ike's health (which was excellent, apart from periodic bouts of a painful stomach upset that was eventually diagnosed as ileitis). There was also Telek, Ike's Scottish terrier. Jim Hagerty, Ike's press secretary at the White House, said that "being President Eisenhower's press secretary was as easy and likeable a job as you could possibly imagine." He made things cozy. At his very first press conference, he told the reporters: "You are quasi members of my staff. Part of the team."

In London, Ike found he had been booked into a suite at Claridge's, the hotel that catered to heads of state and royalty. He immediately transferred to the Dorchester, which was the hostelry where all the action took place (because it had the best and busiest air-raid shelter and was the headquarters of London's top two hostesses, Lady Emerald Cunard and Lady Sibyl Colefax). Later he took Telegraph Cottage in Kingston upon Thames, about fourteen miles from the U.S. embassy in Grosvenor Square. It had seven rooms and was next to a golf course and pistol-shooting facilities. Ike complained: "I have no home to go to" and "I get no exercise." But he found "life in England is wonderful." The London cabbies were quick to recognize him and he went down well with almost everyone in Britain. Churchill loved him. So did Admiral Andrew Cunningham, the naval chief of staff and hero. Sir Alan Brooke at first thought him "a bounder" for smoking before the loyal toast — a solecism committed by many Americans — but later came round as Ike's superb staff work made itself plain.

Ike's first offensive proposal was shot down. He wanted a landing near Le Havre in Normandy on September 15, 1942, under British command but with two U.S. divisions participating. He estimated the chances of getting the lead division on shore as one in two, and of establishing a six-division beachhead as one in five. Called Operation Sledgehammer, it had only a 20 percent chance of success. Ike added: "But we should not forget that the prize we seek is keeping 8 million Russian troops in the war. To allow Russia to collapse would be one of the greatest military blunders of all history." Sledgehammer, rejected, was succeeded by Operation Roundup, a more ambitious plan that would have ended the war in 1944. But that was rejected too, as almost certain to fail. As Churchill argued, and Ike came to agree, a big U.S. failure of their first major operation would have incalculable consequences for morale, Russian as well as Allied. Stalin thought, like Hitler, that Americans were only good at making money and did not know how to fight. It was essential that the first big U.S. operation should work. So Torch won the day.

This decision settled a number of things, including an abortive plan for Marshall to supersede Ike as commander of the eventual cross-channel invasion. But Ike had to drive Torch to victory first. He transferred his headquarters to Gibraltar, where it was housed in one of the deep underground citadels the British had burrowed into the Rock. He liked his post: "A swell command." At Allied Force HQ (AFHQ), he created a fully integrated staff, both mixed Allies and mixed services. It was the first one in history and Ike insisted on absolute discipline — no interservice or inter-Allied abuse was tolerated. A high-ranking American was sent home on the first plane for using the phrase "a British son of a bitch." The offender: "Aw, come *on,* Ike!" Ike: "My ruling stands." Ike's key appointment was General Walter Bedell Smith, whom he stole from General Marshall, who was most reluctant to let him go, and made chief of staff. Smith was first class and stayed with Ike till the end of the war. One of Smith's attractions was that he got on well with Mamie (she coined the name "the Beetle" for him) and kept her informed about Ike's welfare. He also ensured that Ike wrote to her regularly. In fact, Ike wrote 319 letters to Mamie in wartime — only one dictated. She was so angry he never did it again. Some of these letters are memorable, for though Ike was not by nature eloquent, he was articulate and sincere. On the death, in an air crash, of Admiral Bertram Ramsay, of whom he was very fond, he wrote: "It is hard just to sit and pray. But be of good courage — we must hang on to the faith, and hope — and we must believe in the ultimate purpose of a merciful God."

On October 23, 1942, the African pincer began with General Montgomery's assault on Rommel's Afrika Korps at El Alamein. After a fortnight of intense fighting, by November 4, Rommel was in full retreat. Four days later the Torch landings began. It was by far the largest amphibious operation in history (some said since Xerxes invaded Greece across the Hellespont with two million men, but this is a matter of debate). Without Ike in charge, it would have been a shambles. As it was, he just managed to hold it together. The elements came from forty posts on both sides of the Atlantic, and more than half the force was shipped directly from the United States. After endless heated arguments, nine places were selected for landing, around three major ports. Despite all Ike's efforts — one of his maxims, taught by Marshall, was "keep your HQ as small as possible" — his own headquarters expanded from 150 to 1,500 and eventually to a colossal 10,000. More than 800 people were on a need-to-know basis for Torch. By a miracle, or sheer luck, there were no leaks.

The major problem with Torch, which made Ike's life a nightmare at the beginning, was the French.

It is a sad fact that if we take the Second World War as a whole, more French servicemen were engaged in fighting the Allies than the Germans. Of the four French leaders at this stage, Marshal Philippe Pétain, head of the Vichy operations, was obsessed by the fact that the Germans still held a million and a half Frenchmen as prisoners of war, and he had received specific threats from Hitler as to what would happen to them if Vichy forces gave the Allies help, either in mainland France or in North Africa. Second, there was General Charles de Gaulle. He was nominally on the side of the Allies, but in practice he represented a huge, adamantine column of French pride and obstructiveness, hampering Allied efforts at every stage. By superhuman efforts of self-control and charm, Ike eventually got on reasonably well with de Gaulle — better than any other Allied leader, civil or military — but at this point, he was still learning how to handle him. Then there was General Henri Giraud, who fought de Gaulle tooth and nail for control of the Free French, and was even more obdurate, if possible. Ike spent an entire day arguing with him, which he afterward termed "the longest and most exasperating day of my life." Finally, there was Admiral Darlan, who was actually in charge of all French forces in North Africa. The French navy was far more anti-Allies, or rather anti-British, than the army, and in Darlan's case this was aggravated by the fact that one of his forebears had been killed by the British at Trafalgar. Darlan was devoid of honor and had a vicious record of collaborating with the Nazis — he had been particularly assiduous in handing over French Jews to the SS.

Ike, with his strong sense of realism and his instinct for the point that mattered, realized that it was vital to do a deal with Darlan, and he did so. But the deal was leaked before Ike had a chance to make it public himself with his usual spin, and it got him into a great deal of trouble, particularly among people for whom political correctness (a term not yet invented, but the concept was already buzzing around) was more important than men's lives. The nine Torch landings took place on November 8. On November 10, as his part of the deal with Ike, Darlan ordered a cease-fire. On November 11, the deal became public, and all hell broke loose around Ike's ears. But he did not mind so much because by that morning Casablanca, Oran and Algiers were all in Allied hands.

Part of the deal was for French warships based in North Africa to be handed over to the Allies, or better still, to join them with the French crews. But the bitter feelings of the French navy proved too much. Defying Darlan's orders, there was a general scuttling of French warships: three battleships, a carrier, six cruisers, an antiaircraft ship, twenty-eight destroyers and sixteen submarines were all denied to the Allies by November 27. Darlan was assassinated the following month, on December 24.

Torch was enormous, in numbers and geographical spread. A total of more than three hundred warships plus four hundred other major craft were involved, transporting more than 105,000 troops. These were made up of 72,000 from Britain and 33,843 from Virginia under General Patton. What Ike called "some pretty strange supplies" were carried to use as "inducements" for what were expected to be corrupt French officials (and their wives). The bribes included $100,000 in gold, which had to be signed for by Patton, and six tons of women's nylon stockings.

The argument about the landings was over how close they ought to be to Tunis, the nearest port to Sicily and Hitler's means of reinforcing his African armies. The farther from Tunis, however, the less likely they were to be destroyed at sea by German aircraft and submarines. Ike, as he did so often in this and future landings, had to broker a compromise, under which one third of all Allied forces were landed a good thousand miles west of Tunis. At first the plan worked well. The British First Army, led by an aggressive Scotsman, Sir Kenneth Anderson, reached Bône in Tunisia on November 12, and some of his units got to within twelve miles of Tunis in early December. But then the Germans counterattacked. Ike wrote later: "One lesson we had to learn the hard way was the skill, ferocity, and speed of German counterattacks, often from positions we thought impossible." There were some serious American reverses, with heavy casualties, and Ike came under harsh criticism. But it has to be remembered that this was a baptism of fire for the U.S. Army and the U.S. Marine Corps: it was the first serious fighting they had been engaged in since November 1918, nearly a quarter century before. In the end, Tunis did not fall until May 7, 1943, and Axis resistance in North Africa ended only five days later.

But dates do not tell the full story. Once the Torch landings had succeeded, there was never any chance of the Axis powers being able to remain in Africa on a permanent basis. That was Ike's view, and Rommel's too. But Hitler would not admit it. Instead of cutting his losses and getting the Afrika Korps out of Tunis while he could, Hitler continued to pour in reinforcements until the Korps had more than three times as many effectives as Rommel's original expeditionary force. All fell into the Allies' bag.

Torch was expensive. Though the

landings went well, in the end more than 17,000 British and Commonwealth troops were killed or wounded, and well over 10,000 Americans. The number of Germans killed was just over 8,500. On the other hand, by the time the last Germans surrendered at Cap Bon on May 7, there were 166,500 German prisoners in Allied hands, plus 64,700 Italians. Also captured, intact, were 200 German tanks and 1,200 guns. This was the biggest Allied haul of the entire war, and numerically a victory on the scale of Stalingrad, though achieved at a smaller cost. Ike, who had kept his nerve and head — and his temper — throughout some very anxious days, deserved full credit for a campaign that ended in the first decisive Allied victory in Europe, "the biggest hinge of fate," as Churchill called it.

Ike's next aim was to knock Italy out of the war by operating against Sicily. He prepared for this by getting the French to form the Committee of National Liberation, brokering a deal between de Gaulle and Giraud under which both agreed to serve on it. He called this "hard, hateful, and horrible work!" Much easier, by comparison, was taking the key island of Pantelleria, after a massive naval and air bombardment on June 11. A landing on Sicily followed on July 10, which proceeded smoothly, Palermo being occupied on July 22. Sicily was easy meat, or appeared so, but Ike was later criticized for allowing two German divisions to slip over the Strait of Messina, with most of their armor, onto the Italian mainland. But the truth is he was angling for bigger prey: Italy itself. On July 24, in reaction to the fall of Palermo, Mussolini suffered an unexpected defeat at a meeting of the Fascist Grand Council. The king, Victor Emmanuel III, asked Marshal Pietro Badoglio to form a government. Thereafter, Ike was engaged in secret negotiations with the marshal to detach Italy from the Axis cause. His immediate aim was to secure the peaceful surrender of the still formidable Italian navy — unlike the French one, intact.

He succeeded admirably. Eventually five battleships, eight cruisers, thirty-three destroyers, thirty-four submarines and many other craft surrendered, all in full working order, and Admiral Cunningham was able to send a triumphant signal to the Admiralty in London that "the Italian battle fleet is now safely anchored under the guns of the fortress of Malta." Ike, with his strong sense of global strategy, was able to appreciate the wide impact of this switch of allegiance. As he pointed out to General Marshall, it meant the Allies now had sea and air supremacy over the entire Mediterranean. They could land on the southern French coast in tandem with any landings in the north. They could assist the Yugoslavs in the Adriatic. The whole of the Middle East, from Egypt to Persia, was now secure. And Hitler's satellite empire in the Balkans, from Greece to the Ploiesti oil fields in Romania, was now open to Allied penetration.

Against this background, Ike was able to begin the invasion of Italy proper with confidence on September 3, 1943. Five days later, to coincide with massive Allied landings at Salerno, Ike could announce publicly Italy's unconditional surrender, which had actually occurred five days earlier. This was a prelude to Italy's formal declaration of war on Germany, which occurred on October 13. Unfortunately, all this was more a reflection of Italian weakness rather than strength on the ground. The Germans took over Italian positions swiftly and were soon counterattacking with their customary skill and persistence. Indeed, at Anzio they nearly achieved a remarkable success. Ike had to send marine reinforcements to prevent the beachhead from collapsing. In Field Marshal Albert Kesselring the Germans had found a commander whom Ike described as "the coolest and most resourceful of them all." Often outnumbered, Kesselring managed to slow down the Allied advance, and took full advantage of the Apennines to fight a classic defensive campaign.

There was some surprise among the British that Ike was left to handle all the problems of the Italian surrender as well as conduct the military campaign. Churchill solved this conflict by sending out an astute politician, Harold Macmillan, as cabinet minister resident in the Mediterranean, and authorizing him to deal with all political matters on the spot. But provided the military commander had the patience and could find the time to make the political decisions, there was a definite advantage in combining the roles, for at this stage of the war, and particularly in the Mediterranean theater, political and military decisions intermeshed —

as Harold Macmillan put it, they formed "a seamless garment." Ike had the precise talents to switch effortlessly from issuing orders to his subordinate commanders to negotiating with seedy civilian leaders, and then back again. All his previous experience had prepared him for this kind of job. A military success opened up new political possibilities. A political coup might make an entire military campaign unnecessary. We have to bear constantly in mind that Ike regarded the lives of his soldiers as precious. He wanted to spare them. This was a salient consideration in all his calculations. And it was very well known. No Allied commander, in any of the theaters of war, was so eager to avoid casualties by scaling down the intensity of the campaigns, or avoiding them altogether, if the same ends could be secured by a political arrangement. Ike was always looking for political windows through which he could enter by agreement rather than the force of brutal military power.

He also looked for easy geographical pickings that brought major strategic fruits. On September 10, Montgomery's Eighth Army took Taranto in the south of Italy. Ike promptly reinforced this success by pushing the First Division of the Canadian army north to take all the airfields that surrounded Foggia. Their long runways would accommodate the Flying Fortresses of the U.S. Army Air Forces and the Lancasters of Britain's Bomber Command, both of which had the range to strike at a vast number of new targets in central Europe. Henceforth the Allies usually had air superiority in southern Europe, which included most of Italy. It is, however, a curious fact that the weather in Europe, in the second half of 1943 and almost all of 1944, was phenomenally bad, at least in terms of military operations, which counterbalanced Allied air superiority. Montgomery said the weather in Italy, turning the Apennine foothills into oceans of mud, was the worst in his entire military career, more inhibiting than the Flanders mud of Passchendaele, which he experienced in 1917. But the muggy "no-fly" weather of 1943–44 was more decisive because on so many occasions it kept Allied aircraft grounded. There were more than two hundred days when no significant air support for ground troops was possible, and Ike's diaries are full of complaints about the weather. "This weather is intolerable. . . . I am exhausted by news of bad weather. . . . The weather makes everything twice as difficult."

Ike's letters to Mamie also complain bitterly of the weather. But he contrived, always, to strike a note of hope for her sake: "We are hammering away. Regardless of setbacks, disappointments, and everything else, we are on the road to Victory! What a boon peace will be to this poor old world." It was one of Ike's aims, in writing to her so frequently, to fight off the depressions that he knew hit her when he was far away, and all his letters contained, or ended with, a gleam of uplift. Happily, it was his nature. Of all the Allied commanders, military and political — Roosevelt and Churchill, de Gaulle and Marshall, Brooke and Portal, Tedder and King, Cunningham and Ramsay — Ike was easily the most consistently optimistic. Oddly enough, it was the reason why he liked his Irish driver, Kay Summersby, so much — she was "a cheerful soul," as he put it. A friend (probably Beetle Smith) discouraged rumors about their relationship, saying "Leave Kay alone. She's helping Ike to win the war." And it was true. She'd get him to laugh before breakfast. She could even make jokes about the weather: "It's much worse than this in County Cork!" The famous war correspondent Alan Moorehead, who once considered writing a volume on the influence of good humor on warfare, said he would put Ike and his grin on the cover: "You had only to see him grinning to feel a lift of the spirits."

Up until the autumn of 1943 there was still a chance that Marshall or Brooke would be appointed head of Operation Overlord. Each had carried the burden of global oversight for years. Both deserved the chance to show their skills of command in what was clearly to be the greatest seaborne operation in military history. But Marshall never could work up enthusiasm for any operation. He tended always to see the dangers and drawbacks. Brooke had more specific objections to Overlord, which he thought ought to be postponed further until the Allies had enough landing craft to put fifteen divisions on the beaches the first day. He was a ferocious Ulsterman whose overwhelming passion — it amounted almost to a mania — was that most passive and gentle of sports, birdwatching. But he could not see Overlord succeeding as things stood in 1944. The only Allied general who believed in it, apart from Ike, was Montgomery, another born optimist. But Monty was a superbly experienced fighting soldier, not a staff officer of genius. He was given overall command of the fighting units during the initial phase of the invasion — at Ike's suggestion and insistence, the perfect choice. But Ike himself was the obvious and, indeed, the only man to be in charge of everything. He had proved himself in the Mediterranean command. He had never lost confidence, during some extremely hazardous moments, and had always exuded optimism. Moreover, he had learned a great deal, especially about choosing men, and he knew how to apply the lessons. In December he was appointed by FDR and Churchill, with the full approval of Brooke and Marshall, Supreme Commander, Allied Expeditionary Force in Europe, and promptly set up his headquarters (SHAEF) in London.

■ ■ ■ ■

PART THREE: THE DESTRUCTION OF NAZI GERMANY

■ ■ ■ ■

The tide of the war against Hitler turned with the victories of El Alamein and Stalingrad. The success of the campaign to clear the Nazis out of the Mediterranean, and the great tank battle of Kursk, both in 1943, were clear signals that Hitler could no longer win the war and that he ought to seek any reasonable peace he could get. But such was no longer on offer. The Allies had agreed on nothing less than unconditional surrender, and

Ike had already forced those terms on Italy, and had them accepted on September 3, 1943.

Ike was not originally consulted about the unconditional surrender terms, which were essentially FDR's doing — Churchill disliked what he called absolutes in war. But Ike agreed with the principle. Why? Such terms, it could be argued, were bound to prolong the fighting, and so the casualties. But Ike could argue that the failure to beat Germany absolutely in 1918 made possible the Hitler myths on which the Second World War was based. It was "an unnecessary war," as Churchill said, and a prime aim of the Allies now was to ensure that a third world war could not possibly take place. Ike saw the Hitler regime as the absolute of evil, and he was clear about two things: the need to apply what was later called denazification and the punishment of war crimes. Once he became supreme commander, he set up a unit to collect and collate evidence of Nazi atrocities. It proved invaluable and Ike studied its findings, which filled him with disgust. He also became aware, as early as 1942, of Hitler's "final solution," and what was happening in Poland, where Nazi extermination camps were operating. As he wrote to Mamie: "What is going on in German-occupied Europe, under the cover of war, almost defies belief, and makes me glad that I am in a position, or will be, to punish it. I have never believed in revenge, but I have the strongest possible belief in justice, and the need to impose it on evil-doers. We are engaged in a crusade."

The successful invasion of German-occupied Europe and the destruction of Hitler's regime were to be Ike's contribution to this crusade, and the Battle of Normandy his key moment in history. Unlike Marshall and Brooke, Ike believed 100 percent in the necessity of Operation Overlord. The British had built up Bomber Command into a tremendous force in the days when it was the only way to hit back at Nazi Germany. Air Marshal Arthur "Bomber" Harris, its commander, believed, or said he did, that it was a war-winning weapon that could compel a German surrender by sheer destructiveness and killing. The really heavy raids on Berlin and other cities began on February 28, 1943, and continued to mount in scale and intensity. On January 20, 1944, 2,300 tons of bombs were dropped on Berlin alone, and from March 6, these nighttime attacks were joined by daylight attacks on Berlin by the Americans. In April 1944, 81,400 tons of bombs were dropped on Germany. But there was no evidence, so far as Ike could see, that bombs were undermining Germany's resolution to fight on. As he put it, "Only the infantry in

German cities can bring down the Swastika."

Ike recognized that Overlord would be a highly risky venture. In the second half of 1943, the Nazis doubled the number of slave laborers working on the West Wall to more than two million. The blockhouses were almost unbelievably strong and deep, so much so that the French after the war despaired of demolishing some of them, and they are still there. Ike believed that if the West Wall was fully manned, it could not be taken by a seaborne assault. Happily, the Germans did not have the men to defend properly the entire thousand-mile stretch. This opened the way to a deception plan, and as soon as he took over the command, Ike worked hard on this project, which entirely suited his love of deception and deviousness.

As Ike was taking over in London, Rommel was taking over Army Group B of the Wehrmacht, which had been given the job of repelling Overlord. Rommel believed the invasion had to be defeated on the beaches. If the beaches were lost, the Allies would win the battle of France, and with it the war. His overall boss, Field Marshal Gerd von Rundstedt, disagreed, and argued for a defense in depth, with a huge reserve for counterattacks. This disagreement was never re-solved — point one in the Allies' favor. Hitler believed the invasion would come in Normandy and continued to urge his generals to base the bulk of their forces there. And he was right. But all his generals, without exception, thought the Pas de Calais area would be chosen and that the bulk of the reserves must be kept there.

This was well known to Ike through the decryptions of top Wehrmacht signals made available by decoding the Enigma system. Hence the object of his deception plan was to reinforce the view of the German generals that the invasion would come in the extreme corner of northwest France. In fact, there were two deceptions, Fortitude North and Fortitude South, because it was important to make the Germans think invasions were possible and even likely in Normandy, Denmark, Holland and Belgium, as well as in the wrong part of France. This meant twenty German divisions were kept in the wrong country and the strategic reserve was stationed in the Pas de Calais. The deception took many forms. Bombing and reconnaissance flights over Normandy were deliberately limited. Evidence of an (imaginary) army group under General Patton (in temporary disgrace for slapping a soldier's face in a hospital) was created on the coast just opposite Calais; an actor impersonating Montgomery was sent to Gibraltar; and a dead body complete with fake plans was planted where the Germans would find it. Evidence emerged only in 2013 that General Franco, eager to ingratiate himself with the Allies now that he was convinced they were winning, helped with this part of the deception, which was particularly successful. Both Fortitudes, and a third, known as Bodyguard, contained hundreds of different elements, and continued during the actual D-Day and for three weeks afterward, until the German generals finally concluded that they had been taken in. More than half a million Germans remained inactive in the Pas de Calais area.

Ike had been concerned with planning for an invasion of Europe as far back as September 1941, before the United States even entered the war. Once he took over in December 1943, he took an active, direct and detailed part in the preparations. He backed unreservedly the scheme to lay an oil hose on the seabed of the English Channel from the Isle of Wight to Cherbourg, despite its expense and much opposition from various "experts." He was worried that the choice of Normandy, which had his enthusiastic support, meant that a major port, like Antwerp, was unlikely to become available for resupplying until D-Day plus forty, even if all went well. The Pipeline Under the Ocean, or PLUTO, made up for it, at least in part. Some 180 million gallons were pumped through it. Ike also backed an even more expensive scheme to create artificial quays, known as Mulberry harbors, which were towed across the Channel and sunk off the invasion beaches. These required up to a million tons of concrete and two million tons of steel supports, and more than thirty thousand skilled engineers were employed in setting them up. This was just the kind of thing Ike loved to supervise, and to work out the logistics in military terms.

Ike played a major part in supervising the Battle of Normandy right up to the actual invasion. It was originally scheduled for May, but he and Monty pushed it to June to enable landing craft used in the Sicily and Italian operations to be brought from the Mediterranean. Ike increased the power of the first assault from three to five divisions. The scale of Overlord was unprecedented. The total number of troops was more than two million, and nearly 7,000 ships were involved. These included 1,200 warships and more than 4,000 landing craft, made of wood but capable of eight knots. There were 11,500 aircraft deployed, including more than 5,000 bombers and fighter-bombers, which from the first week of May carried out low-level attacks to destroy all main roads, railways, tunnels and bridges in the rear areas, from the Cotentin Peninsula to Calais, to inhibit any movement of German reserves. These raids were designed to reinforce the deception plan.

Ike insisted on the air strikes and also on the presence of a vast naval force to provide bombardments and ensure absolute naval superiority when the first waves went in. So on the first day he used more than five thousand warships, which included five battleships, twenty-three heavy and light cruisers, seventy-nine destroyers and thirty-eight frigates. In the event of losses, eighteen destroyers were held in reserve. The first landings on five main beaches — Utah and Omaha to the west, and Gold, Juno and Sword to the east — were preceded by glider and parachute drops to seize two key bridges. Some 70,500 Americans and 83,115 British and Canadian troops composed this first wave.

Except for Ike and Monty, nearly all the top people were deeply pessimistic about Overlord, although Churchill, to do him justice, was concerned about heavy casualties — he had fearful memories of the Dardanelles — rather than failure. Ike's chief concern was the weather. At the last possible minute he moved the date of Overlord from June 5 to June 6 to secure better visibility. This decision took enormous courage, and even more was required to stick to the revised date, despite much contrary advice.

But both proved quite correct, and June 6, as it turned out, was the best weather day in the first half of the month. Ike called it "by the grace of God my lucky day." On the eve, Churchill took his wife, Clementine, into the Map Room and warned her: "Do you realize that by the time you wake up in the morning 20,000 may have been killed?" Ike's estimate was ten thousand losses. He said: "If any blame or fault attaches to the attempt, it is mine alone." He had personally attended to every main detail of the operation and accepted total responsibility. He wrote a letter of resignation in advance. His last words before the operation began at two a.m. with the landing of six gliders on the Canal de Caen were: "I hope to God I know what I am doing."

He did. D-Day itself exceeded all expectations. Surprise was complete, and on only one of the beaches was resistance fierce. Casualties were much lower than expected. By the end of the second day, 250,000 Allied troops were ashore, plus a great deal of armor. Rommel's assertion — "If we do not defeat them on the beaches the invasion has succeeded and the war is lost" — was proved to be right, then and later. By the morning of June 11, Ike was able to report that all the Allied bridgeheads had been joined "in one continuous front," and that the first phase of Overlord had been successfully completed. Caen was stubbornly held by the Germans and did not waver until July 9. But Monty used it as a fulcrum on which to attract and destroy all the German armor in the area, allowing General Patton's tank forces to break out and plunge deep into France. On July 20, there was an attempt to assassinate Hitler at one of his command posts, and Ike interpreted this as evidence that the more independent-minded German generals had decided that the war was a lost cause and were seeking to replace the Führer with someone who would negotiate with the Allies.

However, the attempt failed and Hitler rounded up the rebel generals and punished them with characteristic ferocity, hanging them with piano wire. The breakthrough in Normandy meant the Germans no longer had a continuous line in the west, and this fluidity was extended when the British landed in the French Riviera on August 15. Ten days later, de Gaulle was able to enter Paris in the wake of Ike's troops and establish his government there. Could the Germans reestablish a continuous line? Of Ike's four chief generals, two, Mark Clark and Omar Bradley, preferred a safety-first policy, advancing on a broad front, with supplies distributed equally between the four Allied army groups, and with the minimum exposure to a German counterattack. Montgomery, in the north, opted for an armored thrust directly into Germany, crossing the Rhine and proceeding to Berlin to wind up the Hitler regime. But this meant he had to have priority for petrol and other supplies. Patton, to the south, also favored a direct thrust, but with the oil and supplies going to *his* group and with the whole of southern Germany as the object.

Ike preferred a broad-front policy, partly because he wanted all four army groups to remain in close touch at all times, partly because he distrusted both Montgomery and Patton on issues of general strategy, believing both were influenced by notions of personal glory, and partly because he wanted to remain on good terms with the Russians, who would see an Allied priority for a thrust on Berlin — or a Patton thrust at Vienna and Prague — as aimed at denying them most of Eastern Europe. In the end, Ike made the decision, firmly, that the front must advance continuously, and both Montgomery and Patton had to submit.

Montgomery later argued in his memoirs that Ike's strategy both ended any chance of finishing the war in 1944 and made his time as president much more difficult by putting Stalin in power in two thirds of Eastern Europe. On the other hand, the German counteroffensive in the Ardennes of December 1944 showed that the Germans were still capable of formidable operations even at this late stage of the war. The possibility cannot be ruled out that Montgomery might have been cut off and surrounded by a German blow east of the Rhine if he'd been allowed to charge on by himself. The same might have happened to Patton, of course, but he could not take part in the later debate because he died as the result of a car accident in 1945.

Ike knew he was bound to win eventually after the success of the Normandy campaign, and there was much to be said for his preferring the strategy of safety rather than risk. It was no easy job to run a quartet of force commanders. Ike himself commented: "Successful generals tend to have a feminine streak and behave at times like operatic prima donnas." Mark Clark was just as vain as Montgomery, though less disobedient. Even Bradley, in Ike's opinion, sometimes lost men for the sake of a tactical gain of little importance. Ike was one of the few American generals who put the lives of his troops before any other consideration — except ultimate victory. General Francis "Freddie" de Guingand, Montgomery's sidekick, who had conciliatory powers rivaling Ike's own, always in the last resort prevented a breakdown of communications between Monty and Ike by appealing to their mutual regard for low casualties. Ike particularly liked Monty's pep talk to soldiers that began: "Now, men, what's your most precious possession?" In response to replies such as "My rifle, sir," he said: "No, you fool, *your life.*" I once asked a senior officer (who was in the Eighth Army from El Alamein right through to the final surrender of the Nazis) who was the best general to serve under. He replied: "The two I had: Monty as my C in C and Ike as my Supreme Commander, to keep Monty under control. That way I stayed alive."

Montgomery always backed down before Ike when it came to a point. He always knew that if Ike told the Chiefs of the Combined Staffs (who had the ultimate authority) that "it is Monty or me," then Ike would win for certain. Thus he signaled to Monty: "I would deplore the development of such an unbridgeable gulf of conviction between us that we would have to present our differences to the CCS. But I am prepared to do it unless you give way. The confusion and debate that would follow would certainly damage the good will and devotion to a common cause that have made this Allied Force unique in history." Montgomery exorcised his anti-Ike demons by grumbling to Brooke: "Ike has never commanded anything before in his whole career. Now, for the first time, he has elected to take direct command of a very large-scale operation and he does not know how to do it." Brooke, for his part, took out his frustrations on his diary: "No one is running the land battle. . . . Eisenhower is on the golf links at Rheims." It is true that Ike had established his advanced head-quarters, with tents and trailers, at the Reims Athletic Club. But he never played golf there — there was no time. Throughout the battle in the west he worked his usual "full duty" hours of six a.m. to eleven p.m. As for Montgomery, after their rows, he sent Ike handwritten letters of submission. One read: "Dear Ike, you can rely on me, and all under my command, to go all out one hundred per cent to implement your plan." It ended: "Your very devoted and loyal subordinate, Monty." As Ike once said, as overheard by Patton: "Monty is a clever son of a bitch."

As for the success of the Germans in forming a continuous front at the end of the summer, it was probably nobody's fault. The weather was to blame. Nothing slows an advance more surely than continual heavy downpours. As Ike wrote to Marshall: "I am getting exceedingly tired of weather." Ike traveled incessantly, but as he told Mamie, "The weather is so miserable that all my travel is by auto."

Ike was unable to prevent an atmosphere of complacency taking over SHAEF in the autumn of

1944, though he did not share it. It was complacency, especially on the military intelligence side, that allowed the Germans to prepare their Ardennes offensive in secret and launch it on December 16, 1944, achieving complete tactical surprise. On a narrow front they deployed an eight-to-one advantage in infantry and four to one in tanks. This is not so remarkable as it seems, because the Germans were usually more numerous on their western front than the Allies, though by now heavily outnumbered on the east. Ike always found difficulty in reinforcing and resupplying his army until the port of Antwerp was reopened to shipping on November 29. Until April 1945, by which time the German army was losing coherence and breaking up, he was never able to rely on numerical superiority. Throughout the campaign he suffered from a shortage of infantry.

Like everyone else, Ike was surprised by the Ardennes sortie (as he liked to call it). But he recovered his equanimity faster than anyone else and never lost his nerve. Indeed, within twenty-four hours, having studied the air intelligence — the weather had miraculously improved for a spell — he decided the Germans had made a mistake. A letter he wrote on December 17 noted: "If things go well we should not only stop the thrust but should be able to profit from it." He told his generals: "The present situation is to be regarded as one of opportunity for us and not of disaster. . . . What I want to see is cheerful faces round the conference table." He himself remained confident, and the Battle of the Bulge, as it was called, brought out the best in him. General Bradley later wrote: "I never admired Ike more than when he was retrieving the Ardennes débâcle, swiftly and decisively." German casualties, for the first time, were more than twice the Allies', and the closing stages of the battle saw a lot of German surrenders, of entire units. By mounting this offensive, which had no strategic significance, the Germans threw away their chance of conducting a wearing-down campaign in Germany, of the type Kesselring fought in Italy.

To Ike's delight, the Germans compounded their Ardennes error by deciding to fight west of the Rhine, instead of stoutly defending it from the right bank. In the process, twenty of their remaining divisions were completely destroyed. They lost 250,000 prisoners and vast numbers of killed and wounded. Ike recorded: "Great satisfaction that the things . . . I have believed in from the beginning and had carried out in the face of some opposition . . . have heartened so splendidly."

Ike was so relieved at the evident disintegration of the German army that he felt able to take a few days' leave. So far as I can see, he had only three days' leave in total from September 1939 to the spring of 1945, during which he normally worked a day lasting from six a.m. to eleven p.m. However, on March 19, 1945, he, plus Bradley, Bedell Smith and four WACs (members of the Women's Army Corps), including his driver Kay, went to Cannes and stayed four days. Ike spent the first two days sleeping. Afterward, he even refused to play bridge: "I can't keep my mind on cards. All I want to do is sit here and not think." He said afterward, he had never been so tired, mind and body, in his entire life. He was fifty-five.

Ike was much criticized at the

time — and has been ever since — for his handling of the closing stages of the war. In particular, his failure to reach Berlin before the Russians was cited as "Ike's biggest mistake in his entire career." The point is worth examining because Ike seems to have changed his mind. In September 1944, he said in private, "Clearly Berlin is the main prize." But at the time he said this, the Russians were still more than three hundred miles from Berlin. By March 1945, when Ike, to Churchill's disappointment and Montgomery's caustic fury, made the decision not to devote extra resources to a race for Berlin, the nearest Allied units were still two hundred miles from Berlin. The

Russians, by contrast, were only thirty-five miles away, and they had 6 million men in eastern Germany. They certainly lied to Ike, telling him they regarded Berlin, and its capture, as of minor military importance. At the same time, they were allocating 1.25 million men and twenty-two thousand pieces of artillery to its capture.

Ike consulted many of his generals on the dispute. Montgomery was enthusiastic for a drive to Berlin, as he had been all along. But Ike, who was hardly on speaking terms with him at this particular juncture, doubted his motives. "He wants to stage a triumphant entry, as the man who won the war," was his dry comment. Mark

Clark was opposed "because he doesn't see how he can get the credit for it." Oddly enough, General Patton, who wanted to race to Berlin in 1944, had lost interest, and was looking forward to a German last stand in the Bavarian Alps, which Ike would give him the job of annihilating. Ike thought a "Nazi redoubt" in the mountains a possibility. In March 1945, he looked favorably on Patton as "my most adventurous general" and paid him a compliment, which Patton recorded: "General Eisenhower stated that not only was I a good general but also a lucky general, and Napoleon had preferred luck to greatness. I told him that this was the first time he had ever complimented me in the two and a half years we had worked together."

However, the general who carried most weight with Ike was Omar Bradley. From the summer of 1944 on, Ike had taken to consulting Bradley frequently as the most levelheaded of the army group leaders. He usually took his advice, especially if it coincided with his own views. And Bradley was emphatic: "Don't go for Berlin unless you have to." Bradley argued that the city was a pile of rubble and that rubble made the best kind of shelter for a really determined defensive action. "Look what happened at Monte Cassino," he said. Bradley calculated that taking Berlin would add another hundred thousand casualties to Allied losses. "A pretty stiff price for a prestige objective" was his conclusion. Hence, Ike rejected all pleas to give Berlin priority. The same arguments applied to Vienna and Prague. Ike summed up his views in a measured comment to Marshall: "I shall not attempt any move I deem militarily unwise merely to gain a political prize unless I receive specific orders from the Combined Chiefs of Staff." No such orders were ever given.

Two points should be made in Ike's favor. First, his dispositions made a Nazi last stand in the Bavarian Alps impossible, and this may have saved the Allies heavy losses. Second, he ensured that his troops took Lübeck, which had the effect of denying Denmark to the Russians. If Joseph Stalin had been able to set up a Communist state in Denmark, the strategic consequences for the West, particularly in setting up NATO, would have been far more serious than similar regimes in Prague or East Berlin. This point is often overlooked in passing judgment on Ike's conduct in 1945.

Ike always tried to keep emotions out of military decisions. But in 1945 he still felt some warmth for the Russians. The huge battles they had fought with the Germans, and the tremendous losses they sustained, had, he felt, saved countless Allied lives. He bore this in mind in rejecting what he felt would be an undignified race for Berlin. His friend Harry Butcher recorded a discussion about this time between Ike and Harry Hopkins (FDR's envoy) concerning the Russians. Ike, who prided himself on getting on well with everyone, said that "anyone who managed to remain friends with Monty, as I have, should find no difficulty in working with the Russians. Anyway, I intend to try."

This was naïve. By 1952, Ike had come to feel that his views in 1945 were "too idealistic." In any case, his political superiors thought otherwise. Harry S. Truman, who assumed the presidency when FDR died on April 12, 1945, soon took a tough line in response to the intransigence of both Stalin and Vyacheslav Molotov, the Soviet foreign minister, and cut off the Lend-Lease, in which the United States supplied Great Britain, the Soviet Union and other Allied nations with matériel during wartime. Ike did his best to keep on friendly terms with all, but he could not feel anything but dislike for the Germans, even in their moment of total humiliation and misery. He wrote to Mamie, on April 15, 1945: "The other day I visited a German internment camp. I never dreamed that such cruelty, bestiality, and savagery could really exist in this world! It was horrible." He saw to it that as many reporters and British and American troops as possible went to concentration camps to witness the depravities and Nazi atrocities. On May 7, 1945, he took part in the surrender signing by the shattered German authorities. He said: "I should have felt elation, but all I felt was tired, dead beat." He dictated a message to the Chiefs of the Combined Staffs after everyone else at his headquarters had tried and failed to rise, or fall, to the occasion. It read simply: "The mission of the Allied forces was fulfilled at 0241 hours local time, 7 May 1945." Ike managed to grin while the newsreel cameras were on him. Then he slumped, and the glass of champagne he reluctantly drank was flat.

On May 25, Ike shifted his headquarters to the sumptuous offices he had been allocated in the I. G. Farben building in Frankfurt. He noted with disgust: "They should belong to a sultan or a movie star." But he was quietly pleased to get a message from General Marshall on behalf of the War Department: "You have completed your mission with the greatest victory in the history of warfare. . . . Since the day of your arrival in England three years ago, you have been selfless in your actions, always sound and tolerant in your judgments, and altogether admirable in the courage and wisdom of your military decisions. You have made history, great history, for the good of mankind, and you have stood for all we hope for and admire in an officer of the United States Army. These are my tributes and my personal thanks."

There was also a personal tribute from Stalin, given to Averell Harriman, the U.S. ambassador to the Soviet Union: "General Eisenhower is a very great man, not only because of his military accomplishments but because of his human, friendly, kind, and frank nature. Unlike most military men, he is not a grubi."*

*Untranslatable, meaning roughly a coarse person.

■ ■ ■ ■

PART FOUR:
RUNNING A TOP
UNIVERSITY

■ ■ ■ ■

The coming of peace in Europe found Ike very tired, but it brought him no rest. He automatically became commander of the American zone of Germany, charged with intricate, delicate and often distasteful problems. The roundup and punishment of Nazi leaders and their criminal subordinates, and the denazification of the German people, were necessary tasks that he discharged with commendable efficiency and his customary zeal. But they were not tasks for which he felt any relish. The enormous pleasure General MacArthur experienced in running Japan, and refashioning the Japanese state and people along nonmilitaristic lines, was not for Ike. In any case, he did not have the power. He shared his authority with British, French and Russian high commissioners, the latter two of whom were haughty, difficult and sometimes impossible colleagues. The Germans were prostrate, obedient and pathetically eager to please. But Ike was revolted by their submissiveness, coming so soon after their cruel arrogance, the consequences of which were to be seen everywhere in Europe's ruined cities. Ike quoted with approval Churchill's dictum: "The Germans are either at your throat or at your feet," and added his own: "I do not warm to a people it is impossible to trust with freedom of moral action."

Ike came across plenty of evidence that he was probably the most well liked and popular American on earth. Honors and decorations were bestowed on him from all over the world. On June 12, 1945, he came to London to receive a specially designed ceremonial sword, modeled on the one that formed the SHAEF shoulder patch. Ike had seldom worn a sword in his life, except to please MacArthur in the Philippines, and he never wore this one. But it pleased him, and he kept it, and it is preserved in the Eisenhower Presidential Library at Abilene. On the occasion of the sword's presentation by the Lord Mayor of London, Ike made a speech at the Guildhall. It was not long, but he took a good deal of trouble over it, and it succeeded admirably in confirming the affection and respect in which he was held by the British, and Londoners in particular.

Ike was the recipient of many invitations, not least from President Truman, who said to him: "I will help to get you anything you want, not excluding the Democrat nomination for president in 1948." In 1946, during a tour of the Far East, he was a guest of Douglas Mac-

Arthur, who gave a dinner in his Tokyo satrapy for thirty people, all Americans, in Ike's honor. During the meal, MacArthur took him to a private room and said: "Either you or I will be President of the United States before long. I am debarred by my present job which I wish to finish, and by the fact that the Republican Party is an oligarchy, whereas I believe in strong, personal leadership. But, since I am out of the running, you are a sure thing for the presidency." Ike (I am quoting from an account he gave shortly afterward to the columnist Joseph Alsop, as given in his autobiography) countered this remark by insisting: "The military have no business in politics, and anyway I have a feeling that the United States has already given me everything I could possibly hope for or deserve, so I have no intention whatever of running for the presidency." Then — continued Ike — "Joe, do you know what the man said to me? He leaned over, patted me on the knee, and had the nerve to say: 'That's all right, Ike. You go on like that, and you'll get it for sure.' "

This incident enraged Ike at the time. But it made Alsop roar with laughter, and in retrospect it shows a degree of prescience unusual for MacArthur. But at the time it probably reflected Ike's true feelings. He was now chief of staff of the U.S. Army, in Marshall's old post, and his hands were full reducing an enormous conscript force to peacetime levels while leaving the United States capable of facing an increasingly bellicose Soviet Union at the outset of what people were already beginning to call the cold war. Ike took his duties very seriously. In particular, he was eager to show that the country would reward GIs for their wartime service by improving their position in the postwar United States. The GI Bill was not his idea, but he took it up with enthusiasm and it had his full backing. He thought it only just that every serviceman who wished, and who even remotely qualified by intelligence, should attend college at the nation's expense.

It was, perhaps, Ike's identification with the GI Bill (also known as the GI Bill of Rights) that led to demands that he should, after he had served a three-year term as chief of staff, accept the presidency of a leading American college. A dozen or more would willingly have had him. The keenest, however, was Columbia, New York's oldest and biggest university, whose trustees bombarded him with requests. "I do not understand it," said Ike. "I am not what you would call an educated man." But this was to ignore the fact that as a graduate of West Point he already held a bachelor of science, and that his brother Milton was president of Kansas State University before moving on, in 1950, to the presidency of Pennsylvania State University, a large and formidable institution.

The older American colleges or universities had been founded for denominational purposes. The oldest, Harvard, had been created in 1636 to train Puritan ministers; William and Mary (1693) in Virginia to train Anglican ones; and Yale (1701), Congregationalists. "New Light" Presbyterians set up Princeton in 1746, and the Baptists, Brown, or the College of Rhode Island, in 1764. Columbia, originally called King's College, was an Anglican establishment set up by a grant from George II in 1754. Only the Philadelphia College, which became the University of Pennsylvania in 1741, was non-sectarian.

King's, refounded after the American Revolution, was named Columbia when it reopened in 1784. It moved to its present location in Morningside Heights in 1897. From 1902, and for the next forty-three years, Columbia was under the presidency of a great American educator, Nicholas Murray Butler. He transformed it into a top-notch research center and one of the largest universities in the world. The trustees were now eager to secure a world-famous figure with the skills and contacts to consolidate Butler's achievements, and pay for them by expanding its endowments.

To get Ike, the trustees were willing to promise him anything in the way of terms, freedom to discharge other duties consistent with his role as president of the university, and latitude in attending and presiding. What finally persuaded him to accept was their vision of Columbia as not merely a superb academic institution, but a national one as well, turning out young people who were essentially first-class citizens, educated at the highest level to serve their country. This coincided exactly with Ike's notion of what a top university should stand for. The trustees also stressed, and Ike knew it to be true, that he was taking over "New York's intellectual powerhouse," as one of them called it, at a historic moment in America's higher education.

The GI Bill became law when the Servicemen's Readjustment Act passed in 1944, even before the war ended, and it promoted an enormous rise in enrollment numbers at colleges. Between 1944 and 1956, when the program ended, 2.2 million went to colleges and 3.5 million to technical schools, and 700,000 took farming courses. This was at a cost of $14.5 billion, provided by taxpayers. In 1949–50, at the end of Ike's first years as a university president, nearly half a million students received degrees, compared with less than half this number in 1940, the last full year of peace (497,000 as opposed to 216,500). This expansion continued until almost half of all U.S. citizens aged eighteen were going to college, and when Ike became head of Columbia, ten campuses had swollen to take more than 20,000 students each.

Ike, and still more Mamie, were astounded by the size of the world they were entering, its variety and scope, and what was expected of them. The president's house in Morningside Heights seemed to them enormous, so Mamie decided they would occupy only two floors. She was disheartened that after all their wanderings, they still could not live in a house of their own, but while Ike was at Columbia, they looked for and eventually found a retirement home. It was at Gettysburg, in Pennsylvania, and was a farmhouse with a decent spread of land. Ike bought it with the money earned by his book of wartime memoirs, *Crusade in Europe.* He built a new house on the site and it eventually became a fine place they both loved.

Ike did his best to fulfill the hopes the trustees of Columbia had placed in him. He found he was expected to greet and offer hospitality to visiting celebrities — heads of state and governments in particular. Meeting the president of Columbia, especially such a famous man as Ike, was part of the New York tour for grandees. He could play this role very well, but it took up his time. He was also in constant demand by the White House, by the War Department and by the new Department of Defense. Ike had precisely the sort of skills in most request during a period of fundamental reorganization of America's defense, with the coming of nuclear weapons and the assumption of the duty to defend the West at the onset of the cold war. What was to become the North Atlantic Treaty Organization (NATO) was in its early stages, and it was clear Ike would be needed to give it shape and a sense of purpose. All this was happening while he was president of Columbia and supposedly devoting himself to its well-being.

Indeed, of the many criticisms leveled at Ike for his performance as a college president, nearly all of them from academics and members of the faculty, the only one with real validity is that he did not give the job enough of his time. It is notable that the trustees who had appointed him never reproached him on this score, for he had specifically warned them that demands by the federal government might occasionally be irresistible. In fact, Ike gave Columbia all the time he could, but he was careful to allocate it in a productive and intelligent manner — in which he was by long experience an expert. When examined, the complaints by Columbia professors boil down to this: Ike did not see enough of them. In particular, it was difficult to get an appointment to see him, and calling on him without one was impractical. It is a curious fact that tenured professors at most American universities are not particularly eager to spend time with their presidents, and complaints that he or she is sparing of that time are not often voiced. But Ike was world famous, and even left-wing academics — his most vociferous critics — were eager to be photographed with him as proof of their friendship or even intimacy. Ike never needlessly grudged time for a photo session, but he did insist that meetings with individual academics should have a specific and useful purpose. He did on one occasion observe that his academic colleagues tended "to need more time to come to the point than people in the Army," and he went on the record with this definition of an intellectual: "A man who takes more words than is necessary to tell more than he knows."

On the other hand, Ike often, if not always, enjoyed high-powered academic company, and testified at the time: "Living with a distinguished faculty gives me many wonderful hours I could never have in any other environment." He listened hard. He took in what he was told. "He learned with amazing speed," said the senior dean.

Unlike most college presidents, Ike sat in on classes and took part in discussions with students and teachers. He had a definite effect on the curriculum at Columbia. He was especially interested in history and physics, and examined carefully what was taught in both. He made innovations. He thought the university should take a close interest in the efficient use of resources, both human and physical. He had Columbia set up a course on human resources that was the first of its kind at any American college. This was complemented by a course on soil erosion, in which, being from Kansas, he had shown an interest all his life. He wanted to draw attention to the misuse or underuse of any natural resource, and he insisted that this was a priority for any modern university that sought to make a contribution to the life of the nation. This was introduced in 1949–50 and was another innovation. It is worth remembering that Rachel Carson's book *Silent Spring,* which first drew attention to the damage mankind was doing to the world in the heedless pursuit of wealth, was not published until 1962.

Ike was also surprised that in the teaching of history, virtually no mention was made of the twentieth century. He thought it disgraceful that, in a world just emerging from the greatest war in history, nothing was taught about why wars occurred and what could be done to prevent them. The result of his concern was the Institute of War and Peace Studies, another pioneering effort to get the university anchored in the modern age, as opposed to the academic past. He raised the money to endow a chair in competitive enterprise. But probably his most important innovation, and certainly the project dearest to his heart, was what he called the American Assembly, based at Arden House on the Hudson, which brought together academics, business and union leaders, and other opinion formers in a formula designed "to protect democracy from its enemies."

This kind of formula provoked

amusement and even occasional fury among left-wing academics. Others found it naïve and embarrassing. But it was the kind of thing Ike found it his duty to perform. We must never forget his strong sense of duty. It was always pervasive in his life and never stronger than when he was outside the discipline of military service, when he was, as it were, imposing on himself a regimental pattern of his own making. Ike did not mind being accused of naïveté or innocence when he was pursuing what he conceived as America's national interest. Asked about his aims at Columbia, he did not hesitate to proclaim: "Every student who comes to this place must leave it, first, a better citizen, and only secondly a better scholar." "Citizenship," not a word which sprang naturally to the lips of academics, was one he used easily, and it meant a lot to him. He said once: "To be an American citizen is one of the world's great prizes." He believed Americans were insufficiently informed of their duties and responsibilities as citizens. He raised substantial sums of money to finance the Citizenship Education Project. Every citizen was part of what he called the American Team. Teamwork was, as always, all important to Ike, just as important as, perhaps more than, the cultivation of the individual, which he recognized as the dynamic of American enterprise and exceptionalism. Teamwork had been the keynote of his success as a general. It was not an obvious characteristic of an academic community, but Ike saw no reason why it should not become so.

Indeed, he went on the record with one or two lapidary statements about what universities were for. Thus: "I want Columbia to become a more effective and productive member of the American national team." And: "Columbia must have an underlying purpose which far transcends the discovery and imparting of knowledge." This purpose was essentially the same as that which the American armed services existed to pursue and protect, though using quite different means, and it was a noble purpose. Ike did not, and could not, use the language and vocabulary of academic discourse, but he was trying to express the same ideal of university education that the best kind of academic wished to further. It must be said that he did a remarkable amount, in a practical way, to further university ideals in the comparatively short time he held office at Columbia, more than most college presidents achieve in a decade or even a lifetime.

Ike also put Columbia's finances on a firm foundation. His orderly mind made him a natural budget reformer, as he was to prove on a much bigger scale at the White House. He found the way in which the budget was presented at Columbia to be messy and needlessly complicated, and it half concealed a large cumulative deficit. He reformed the budget and in the process eliminated the deficit. Indeed, he raised very large sums of money. Ike had a genius for fund-raising, one of the reasons, of course, that the trustees were so keen to appoint him. As one of them remarked: "Ike extracted millions of dollars from people who did not even know where Columbia was."

Moreover, this devotion to the university's financial well-being continued long after Ike ceased to be its president. At the White House he was instrumental in steering donors and advantages its way. In 1965, after Ike had ceased to be president, Columbia, in its faculty and student numbers, and in its endowments, compared favorably with all but the richest and largest American universities. It had an endowment of $201 million, a faculty of 3,430 and 16,700 students. For purposes of comparison, Yale had an endowment of $335.5 million, a faculty of 2,500 and 8,660 students. Harvard, the richest of all by far, had an endowment of $620 million, a faculty of 5,680 and 11,950 students. Thus, Ike raised Columbia high amid its peers, and left it big, busy and secure.

He also became more secure himself. He had been genuinely apprehensive about his ability to run a top academic establishment, and the fact that he was able to do so, and to get along with students and staff, to master its finances and improve them, and not least to introduce new and useful courses was a tremendous reassurance for him. His health improved, partly because he now regularized his exercise and partly because his stomach cramps were now properly diagnosed as chronic ileitis and appropriately treated. His new doctor, General Howard Snyder, who took charge of his medical treatment, decided he was smoking too much. He ordered Ike to cut down from four packs a day to one. To his surprise and delight, Ike, who had always regarded smoking as an undisciplined and disorderly habit, quit completely, and never smoked again. Friends noticed a transformation in his breathing.

Ike thus passed his sixtieth birthday in fine fettle. He enjoyed being a grandfather. His three grandchildren, John's offspring, were a great delight to him. Mamie was helpful to him at Columbia and busied herself happily at the rebuilt house in Gettysburg. But Ike was never left alone. He was always being sought out for jobs, political and military. Political jobs — to run for U.S. senator in New York, for example — he could turn down. Military challenges were more difficult to resist. In October 1950,

President Truman asked Ike to accept the top command role in the newly created North Atlantic Treaty Organization, as Supreme Allied Commander, Europe (SACEUR). Ike insisted that Truman's original "request" should be changed to "order"; then he accepted. This meant transferring to NATO headquarters outside Paris, and another unexpected move for poor Mamie. In fact, Ike's hesitation in accepting the new job was chiefly occasioned by worries about Mamie, who had heart trouble about this time. But as Ike put it, "SACEUR is the most important military job in the world," and he knew he had exactly the right qualifications for the first holder of the appointment.

The Columbia trustees, however, insisted that he take a leave of absence instead of resigning.

Ike returned to Europe in January 1951. He left Columbia, he said, "with regret, but in eager anticipation at taking up my new task." He saw it largely in military terms. He was not an ideologue. He had hated Nazi Germany because of its deeds — and what he had seen — but he had no such feelings about Russia. He had never read Marx any more than he had read Hitler's *Mein Kampf*. At Columbia, he opposed appointing known Marxists to teaching jobs because they might introduce "alien and untrue" material into their lectures and seminars. He said he agreed with President Charles Seymour of Yale when he announced: "We do not intend to hire communists here." In 1949, he joined President James Conant of Harvard on a panel of top academics that ruled that committed Communists were "unfit" to teach at American universities. But there was never anything bitter or obsessive in his attitude. He was not interested in political ideas except insofar as they had practical import. He thought university professors should not have a secret agenda in their teaching. Equally, he thought that the Soviet Union had far too many divisions in central Europe, and that it was right for the Western powers to combine to face the potential threat that these divisions, by their very existence and position, inevitably posed.

Ike took a severely practical view of the role of NATO land forces. They ought to be sufficiently strong to slow down any Russian incursion and "impose a pause" to give both sides time to consider the implications of what was happening. He did not believe the USSR would deliberately embark on a third world war in an age of nuclear weapons, any more than the United States would. But there was a real risk that both sides might blunder into one. NATO existed to make such a blunder impossible.

But for this reason it needed an

efficient command structure and enough fighting units to be taken seriously. All its members needed to contribute, according to their wealth, population and geography. At his first NATO meeting, Ike found an atmosphere of confusion and unreality. He banged the table, as he knew well how to do. His message was: "Stop moaning, and get down to business." It is fair to say that he had an electrifying impact. He was rough with the French, the Danes and the Dutch, accusing them of "fooling around" and "wasting time." Ike was capable of notable if simple speech when roused, and his utterances during his early days at NATO were described as "superbly eloquent." He held a press conference in Germany that was "a real eye-opener" and "the right kind of shock-tactics." Having determined what was really needed in Europe, he returned briefly to the United States and addressed a joint session of Congress on February 1, 1951. It was one of the most important speeches he made in his life, and Ike showed himself far more effective at presenting the NATO cause than any member of the Truman administration. He said that "the future of civilization is at stake." He insisted that "the first line of defense of the United States is on the Elbe." He argued that "one dollar spent in Europe is worth four dollars spent in the United States." After Ike's appearance before Congress, there was never any doubt that America would support the NATO concept and provide its lion's share of the funds. He had the same effect elsewhere. On July 3, 1951, he addressed a great gathering of the English-Speaking Union at London's Grosvenor House. An audience of 1,200 key British personalities heard him in rapt silence, then gave him an enthusiastic standing ovation. Churchill called it "one of the greatest speeches delivered by any American in my lifetime." On the right occasion, to the right people, and suitably uplifted by the importance of what he had to say, Ike was an admirable speaker.

These two notable orations had

far-reaching consequences. They provoked the query: When Ike has set up NATO as he wishes, why should he not go on to become president of the United States?

■ ■ ■ ■

PART FIVE:
A FAIR
CAMPAIGN FOR
THE WHITE
HOUSE

■ ■ ■ ■

Given the American tradition of electing successful generals as presidents — a tradition formed by George Washington, Andrew Jackson and Ulysses S. Grant — there was always a strong chance, some would rate it a certainty, that Ike would run. He said no many times. Did he mean it? Who can say? He did, and he did not. He disliked political generals. He disliked putting himself forward. He once said: "I want to be as unlike Douglas

201

MacArthur as possible." He might have said the same about George Patton. Ike must have known he had remarkable qualities, including those well suited for high office in the civilian sphere. But he was overwhelmingly eager that they should be "discovered," rather than presented by himself, something inseparable from running for the White House. It was not so much a question of seeking the limelight. Ike never did that. It was, rather, waiting for the limelight to come to him.

On the other hand, he had an unspoken rule that he must never decline when duty unmistakably called. The United States at mid-century was unarguably the most powerful nation on earth. It was the largest petroleum producer in the world and supplied more oil than the rest of the world's nations together. It harvested one third of the world's grain and half its cotton. It was the world's largest producer of phosphates, iron ore, zinc, lead, copper, salt and precious metals, including uranium. It had 90 percent of the world's natural gas production. In metals, the United States outproduced the combined output of Germany, the USSR, Venezuela, Japan, France, Iran, Poland, Britain, the Netherlands, India, Burma and Belgium. Its production of minerals was four times that of the second largest producer, the Soviet Union, and larger than the combined output of the seven major producers. Almost half of the world's manufactured goods came from the United States. Between 1940 and 1945, the American gross national product doubled, and the ranks of the U.S. Army increased to 8.2 million, with more than 12 million on active duty in all the services. This was more than Russia or the entire British Empire. On January 1, 1946, the U.S. Navy had 70,579 ships, a much larger navy than the entire rest of the world combined, comprising 13,828,000 tons. There were 72,726 planes in the U.S. Air Force, plus 40,000 in the Navy, far more than the rest of the world could muster. All this power was centered in the White House, and effectively wielded by the president, the one man in the nation for whom everyone had the power to vote. It was inconceivable to Ike that a clear call to run for this incomparable office could be resisted.

By the beginning of the 1950s, this call was increasingly insistent and from a variety of quarters. Hitherto, entries in Ike's diaries had been consistently negative: "I will not run under any circumstances." From 1950 the tone changed. The Truman administration fell into deep disrepute. The Republican Party appeared the prisoner of a diehard faction headed by Senator Robert A. Taft,

"Mister Republican," as he was known. Polls showed that an Eisenhower candidacy would attract broad cross-party support. Ike did not trust polls at this stage in his career, but he listened to his friends. There was a tight little group of them, with whom he played golf at Augusta, Georgia, and who were known to one another as "the Gang." They were all very wealthy men. There was Clifford Roberts, a financial manager, who advised Ike on his investments. A stock-market wizard, he made Ike rich. Bill Robinson, publisher of the *New York Herald Tribune,* served Ike as his close adviser on the details of politics. Ellis D. Slater, president of Frankfort Distillers, was a rumbustious organizer of dinners and luncheons, whose wife, Priscilla, became Mamie's best friend. Other regular members of the Gang were W. Alton Jones, president of the Cities Service oil corporation, and Robert W. Woodruff, chairman of Coca-Cola. All were Republicans. The only Democrat in the group, by birth rather than conviction, was the corporate lawyer George Allen, perhaps the shrewdest of the group, who had the gift of making Ike laugh uncontrollably. It is a notable fact that Ike, brought up in a family of boys, much preferred the collective company of men. He was never at ease with women, except individually. All-male camaraderie suited him best, especially when centered round a game like golf (or even bridge). All these men played golf regularly at the Augusta National Golf Club, and together they built Ike a cottage just off the course. They were unanimous that Ike had a duty to the nation to run in 1952. They viewed with horror any continuation of a corrupt Democratic regime, but they saw the current alternative, a reactionary Taft administration, as equally distasteful. They saw a liberal Republican government of the kind Ike would run as exactly what the nation and the world needed: a balanced budget, a firm line with the Soviets, low taxes and a probusiness approach to spending, with a generous attitude to America's friends in the world and a willing hand stretched out to any country whose democracy was under threat. One of them had Ike's two key speeches, in London and to the joint session of Congress, reprinted as a pamphlet. This was circulated in huge quantities and served as a kind of manifesto of an Ike presidency. Ike, for his part, never took the role of candidate. He did not exactly protest every step to the White House, but he never said anything specifically in favor of running until he was a declared candidate. On the other hand, he received countless invitations to speak all over the country, and those he accepted, on the advice of Bill Robinson, reflected the audience and spread of localities of someone in a pre-campaign mode.

Ike also circulated among opinion makers and the influential. His big grin, his firm handshake, the impression he gave of determination and enthusiasm for the country, were enormously impressive and became hallmarks of his public style long before he started to campaign actively. Whatever his inner thoughts — and he was not a man who easily divulged them — he gave the impression of someone who would accept the presidency only from a strict sense of his duty. This was, though I think not deliberately, exactly the manner in which George Washington had approached the job in the 1780s. Ike never made the comparison himself. But he liked it being made by others. He used to repeat the story of King George III's asking Benjamin Franklin: "What will General Washington do now that the war is over?" and Franklin replying: "Oh, I think he will return to his farm." Whereupon the king said: "If he does that, he will be the greatest man alive." Ike felt that it was right to strive for such an office — that is, to campaign actively and openly — only when imperative duty commanded. That might be so in his case if the alternatives were obviously against the national interest, as they increasingly appeared to be.

Ike came from a natural Republican background in Abilene, and most of the senior officers with whom he had mixed in recent years were Republican voters, unless there were strong family reasons for voting Democratic. He had never registered a party affiliation or voted in a federal election. He once divulged that if he *had* voted, he would have backed the Republican Party in 1932, 1936 and 1940, and the Democrats in 1944, but gave no reasons for these choices. The Republican Party was his natural home, but one he did not choose to frequent. In 1950–51, he came under increasing pressure from Republican liberals to oppose the right wing, and at the same time to offer serious opposition to another

Democratic victory. Henry Cabot Lodge Jr., senator from Massachusetts, led a group of Republican internationalists who set up a network campaigning for Ike in New England. The first "I Like Ike" badges began to appear. At the same time, the governor of New York, Thomas Dewey, who had been surprisingly beaten by Truman in 1948, begged Ike to save America "from going to Hades in the handbasket of paternalism-socialism-dictatorship."

Ike had no gut feelings about domestic policies, other than wanting a balanced budget. But he hated isolationism, which he held to be responsible for the Second World War. Taft stood for everything he disliked in politics, including opposing the NATO form of collective security with which he was now identified. If any one emotion pushed Ike into running in 1952, it was hostility to Taft. He told one of his Gettysburg friends: "Taft is a very stupid man. He has no grasp of the big issues in the world today, and no intellectual ability. As President he would be a disaster but he will never make it. He will be beaten for sure." Dislike of Taft led him to agree to let his name be put forward among the Republican contenders in the New Hampshire primary in March 1952. He did not make any declarations. In fact, he was still in Europe at the time. He was not, he said, campaigning. Yet he emerged a clear winner: 46,661 votes against 35,838 for Taft, and derisory scores for other contenders.

This proved to be the turning point. Taft had worked systematically and over a long period for victory in New Hampshire, and the fact that Ike had been able to beat him decisively without lifting a finger made it clear he was a national winner. The more intelligent Republican organizers and financial backers now saw the choice as between Taft, with whom many agreed, and Ike, who could actually win. The cash began to flow Ike's way.

As a politician, Ike was perhaps the most enigmatic figure of the twentieth century. Commentators, academic historians and, for a long time, all the "experts" gave him a low rating in skills. In 1962, after he left the presidency, a poll of historians rated him twenty-first out of thirty-four American presidents. In 1983, a similar poll judged him ninth. In the twenty-first century, estimates ranged from sixth to third best. This was consistent with an upward revision of the "Eisenhower decade" — the 1950s — in American history. By 2012, this was seen as "perhaps the most successful decade in the whole US story," in great part due to Ike's careful handling of events in the White House.

Those who got Ike wrong invariably did so by underestimating him. They zero rated his intelligence. They thought him inarticulate and tongue-tied. They believed him lazy and afraid of hard work. They found him a stranger to craft and cunning. They believed he relied entirely on associates and underlings to do the hard work, to give him crucial advice and to steer him off foolish decisions. They were wrong on all these points. Ike was highly intelligent, knew exactly how to use the English language, was extremely hardworking and very crafty indeed. In practice, he made all the key decisions, and everyone had to report to him on what they were doing and why. Ike did not exactly choose to mislead people about his abilities, but when they underrated him, he certainly made no attempt, as a rule, to correct their impression. He seems to have found it convenient and useful for people to get him wrong. He chuckled within himself.

Of course, the really able knew that Ike was first class. Field Marshal Bernard Montgomery learned by experience that Ike knew how to work any system in which he found himself in charge: "He has this power of drawing the hearts of men towards him as a magnet attracts the bits of metal. He has merely to smile at you, and you trust him at once." A key to both Ike's deviousness and his extraordinary ability was his press conferences. If he had things to hide or was unsure about, or needed to play down, he took refuge in a curiously elastic form of "verbal glutinosity" (as Joseph Alsop termed it), which aroused much laughter and sneering and was widely imitated by reporters and opponents who did not realize that the joke was on them. Yet the real experts could spot a master. FDR's press secretary, Steve Early, went to one of Ike's first press conferences and called it unequivocally "the most magnificent performance of any man at a press conference that I have ever seen. He knows his facts. He speaks freely and frankly, and he has a sense of humor, he has poise, and he has command."

Anyone who had taken the trouble to glance at Ike's military record in detail could not possibly have fallen into the error of thinking him capable of muddled English. He had written position and situation papers of every kind at all stages of his career as a staff officer, and all were in beautiful English. They can be seen in his presidential papers. All intelligent observers who had rated Ike a booby from the 1950s, and for long afterward, were eventually forced by the facts and by the publication of secret papers, phone logs and transcripts — and not least by clever men who had been hoodwinked — to revise their judgments. Among them was Arthur M.

Schlesinger Jr., the historian of the Kennedy era that swiftly followed on Ike's time, and whose brilliance and luminosity he had originally contrasted with "the dim obtusity and leaden language of Eisenhower and his gruesome followers." He was forced to admit, in a revisionist report in 1983, a decade and a half after Ike's death, that newly released papers "showed much more energy, interest, self-confidence, purpose, cunning, and command than many of us had supposed in the 1950s." Schlesinger found him "the dominant figure in his administration whenever he wanted to be (and he wanted to be far more often than he seemed at the time); and that the very genius for self-protection that had led him to exploit his reputation for vagueness and muddle and to shove associates into the line of fire obscured his considerable capacity for decisions and control."

Another liberal revisionist, Murray Kempton, praised Ike's political intelligence as "outstanding," adding: "He was the great tortoise shell upon whose back the world sat for eight years. We laughed at him; we talked wistfully about moving; and all the while we never knew the cunning beneath the shell." Others came to regard him as one of the cleverest operators who ever occupied the White House, "a consummate tactician who also had a profound feeling for strategic objectives."

Strangely enough, Ike took readily to the political schizophrenia needed to keep the Republican Party united until the election was over. He took little interest in the platform drafted by the hard-liners at the party convention. He knew that the ideas of "liberating" Eastern Europe and "repudiating Yalta" were nonsense, as nobody intended to do anything in practice about what was popularly known as "roll-back." The "captive peoples" of Europe would stay captive except for Republican rhetorical purposes. Drafting Ike on this ticket made no sense, but it did not matter. Ike bowed to the pundits and agreed to the choice of Richard Nixon as his running mate to give balance to the platform. Nixon was only thirty-nine and looked young, whereas Ike at sixty-two was old to be running for the presidency for the first time. Ike never warmed to Nixon, but Mamie liked him. He was also a first-class campaigner and swung over to Ike many delegates in his own state, California, where Ike was supposedly weak. The convention was bitter, and it was thanks to Nixon that Ike got the nomination and, after long arguments, the Taft forces were persuaded to work for him in the campaign. Nixon spoke their language. He hated Adlai Stevenson, the Democratic candidate, for reasons buried deep in the sinister depths of class, prejudice and privilege, and joined with Senator Joseph McCarthy of Wisconsin, now emerging as a malign force in American politics, in labeling the governor of Illinois as "soft on communism." Nixon called him "Ad-Lie," and "Adlai the Appeaser" who "had a Ph.D. from Dean Acheson's Cowardly College of Communist Containment." "What this country needs," Nixon intoned, "is a khaki-clad president, not one clothed in State Department Pinks." There were a lot of sly allusions to Stevenson's supposed lack of masculinity. He was "Adelaide," with "a certain fruitiness about him," and was sometimes made to "seem like a genteel spinster who got the elocution prize at Miss Smith's finishing academy."

Ike had nothing to do with this skullduggery. On the other hand, he did not repudiate it. In the campaign of 1952, he sometimes appeared hesitant, uncertain and even cowardly. He was self-confident, as he always was, but he lacked the authority of elected office and did not know how far he could go in rejecting extremists in his own party, at least publicly. There came one moment of ignominy — the only one in his entire career — when he bowed to pressure in a manner that left him deeply ashamed for the rest of his life. On a visit to McCarthy's

stronghold, Wisconsin, he was persuaded — by one of the Gang,
probably Robinson — to delete
from a speech a paragraph praising
the loyalty and patriotism of his old
boss, General George Marshall,
who had come under attack, notably from Senator William E. Jenner. Ike hated Jenner, one of the
few Republicans he could not share
the same room with. "I cannot bear
to shake that man's hand," he said.
"I feel dirty from the touch of the
man." That was strong language
from Ike, who was sparing of verbal
extremism. But Jenner had called
Marshall "a front man for traitors."
Unfortunately McCarthy heard of
the deletion and had both versions
of the speech circulated to the

press. It rightly brought Ike accusations of spinelessness, and a public reference to "lack of backbone" by Stevenson. Ike regretted it immediately and never forgave himself. Before this episode and after, he often paid tribute to Marshall's patriotism, but the damage was done and could not be repaired. It was a moment of turpitude and brought home to Ike the painful cost of politics in a way nothing else could have done. He refused to talk about it — ever.

There was another moment in the campaign when Ike felt the burden of guilt. It concerned Nixon, whom he could never like. It may be that Ike had an instinctive feeling for the faults of character that much later embroiled Nixon in the Watergate business. Certainly Nixon's aggressive campaigning aroused the vicious enmity of certain radical journalists on the White House circuit, who never let up in their determination to "get" Nixon. The 1952 campaign was their first big opportunity. They discovered Nixon was the beneficiary of a certain private campaign fund. It was not large — $15,000 — and was perfectly legal, but they contrived with headlines and extrapolated quotations to make it sound corrupt. The fact that Stevenson also had access to (several) such funds was ignored. Ike read the reports and was said to have remarked: "We must be as clean as a hound's tooth." Nixon was angry that Ike did not immediately come to his defense, and made the mistake of phoning Ike and using a phrase that Ike found deeply disgusting: "There comes a time in matters like this when you've either got to shit or get off the pot." This phrase, and still more the repulsion it aroused in Ike, who was squeamish in some ways, pointed to a bottomless cultural gulf between Ike and his running mate.

Left to himself, Nixon decided to go on national TV and make the speech of his life. He described his family circumstances and possessions in detail, and said, "Pat [his wife] doesn't have a mink coat. But she does have a perfectly respectable Republican cloth coat." He said they had been given a little cocker spaniel by a Texas supporter, which their six-year-old daughter had called Checkers — "And you know, the kids, like all kids, loved the dog, and I just want to say this, right now, that regardless of what they say about it, we are going to keep it." The Checkers speech was a huge popular success, and turned the tide overwhelmingly for Nixon. Ike drove to the airport to meet him with the greeting "You're my boy!" It demonstrated the power of TV, but Ike needed no convincing on this point. True to his military training in always lining up the best technical advice for any operation, he assembled a team of experts for his campaign who insisted on his making the fullest possible use of TV. This included taping forty twenty-second TV shots or "spots" in which he gave short answers to key campaign questions, with "ordinary voters" recorded afterward asking them. These were used over and over again, nationwide, with Ike's campaign funds paying for them. Ike found that the spots brought in more money in contributions than they cost to transmit, and his masterly use of TV, for the first time in an American election — or any election, anywhere — undoubtedly contributed to the magnitude of his victory.

Adlai Stevenson, Ike's opponent,

came from a patrician background, and sneered at Ike's use of TV "to sell him like toothpaste." "This isn't Ivory Soap versus Palmolive," he complained, "but to decide who should occupy the nation's highest office." No one took any notice. Ike's backers spent more than $2 million on the spots, an immense sum at that time, and they became standard fare in every subsequent election. Stevenson was a successful governor in a big, difficult state, but his education — he had been at Choate, Princeton, and Harvard Law School — his accent and manner, and his general air of condescension and remoteness were against him, especially when compared with Ike's wonderful grin and down-to-earth geniality. Ike was a bit wooden at the start of the campaign, but he soon settled down. The "I Like Ike" campaign button was probably the best ever — thirty million were made and distributed. Stevenson was a fine speaker and produced wonderfully polished oratory, but he came over as an intellectual. This appealed to the overwhelmingly liberal press corps but less so to uncommitted voters. Stevenson was bald and the term egghead attached itself to him in a disconcerting manner. One of Ike's gang, George Allen, coined the phrase "Eggheads of the world, unite. You have nothing to lose but your yolks," which was eventually appropriated by Stevenson himself, but not till 1954, after the election had been won and lost. During the campaign, the egghead-intellectual label made Stevenson seem vulnerable and distant, whereas Ike appeared the reverse of intellectual, which helped him.

The election was highly successful and produced an enormous turnout. Stevenson actually received 3,140,000 votes more than Truman did in his successful campaign of 1948, but he could not even carry the "solid South," losing Texas, Virginia, Tennessee and Florida. Ike attracted the largest number of votes in history, almost 34 million, 55.5 percent of the total, against 27 million for Stevenson. He took the Electoral College, by 442 to 89, and on his coattails carried both houses of Congress, the Senate by 48 to 47 and the House by 221 to 213. This immense personal victory, due to Ike's winning personality and vivid, modern style of campaigning, put the Republicans back in charge of the country for the first time in a generation, since 1930 in fact, and introduced the Eisenhower decade in American history.

■ ■ ■ ■

PART SIX:
THE
PRESIDENTIAL
ART OF
BALANCE

■ ■ ■ ■

Ike was sixty-two when he entered the White House — old for the job. On the other hand, he had known Washington well for more than twenty years, much better than most incoming presidents. He was fit. At 175 pounds, his weight was almost the same as when he was at West Point. He was five foot ten, but many people thought him six foot because he held himself so erect. He still got up at six a.m. and continued to do so throughout his eight years in the White House.

He insisted on a complete break with the Truman White House, one of the most ruthless in the history of the presidency. His relations with Truman were at zero point. Truman thought his campaign had been totally dishonest and that Ike had attacked policies in defense and foreign affairs that he had helped to make. Ike, he said privately, was "pinheaded," "chicken-hearted," "essentially a surly, angry, and disagreeable man." He "would make a bad president." Their hand-over meeting was scheduled to last only twenty minutes and in fact took fifteen. Nothing important was said. The clear-out of Truman staffers went right down to low levels and was perhaps the most thorough in White House recollection. Ike was appalled at the inadequacy of records kept during the Truman regime and insisted on an overhaul that imposed the best standards he had known in the army. Every minute of Ike's day was recorded in detail. All phone calls were logged and, if feasible, recorded, and there was a detailed record of all official transactions. The result is that researchers know much more about Ike's White House than Truman's (or FDR's), and the recording systems adumbrated those made notorious during the Watergate scandal.

Access or nonaccess to Ike was a key issue from the earliest days of

241

the new White House. Everybody wanted to see Ike — it was a fact of life. Ike brought with him from his final army days a team consisting of a colonel, two sergeants and four recording typists, the whole supervised by his son, John. At Columbia there had been a system of buzzers and colored lights inviting and tracking visitors into Ike's suite of rooms. This arrangement had worked efficiently from Ike's point of view, but it had outraged some of the academics, part of their general hostility to his "military" management of the university. At the White House, the monitoring control of Ike's movements, visitors, phone calls and contacts was more complex, systematic and, at times, oppressive. There was a sense in which Ike was cut off from the outside world. Every day, before he rose at six a.m., his valet, John Moaney Jr., put out his underclothes, shirt, jacket, pants, shoes and tie. He never dined in a restaurant, drove a car, used a checkbook or handled money, except change for golf or bridge. He hated to lose and settle up: one of his few weak points. All his travel arrangements were made for him. He told a colleague: "Aides have sat on my right all my life."

He took immense trouble selecting his cabinet and senior White House personnel, using army staff methods. He never picked old friends or colleagues. The only exception was Bedell Smith, whom he made undersecretary of state, to balance John Foster Dulles. Ike had a high opinion of Dulles, an old Wall Street corporate lawyer whose experience of diplomacy went back to Woodrow Wilson's day. He was a powerful figure who many people believed was in total charge of U.S. foreign policy under Ike. Nothing could have been further from the truth. Dulles told me himself not long before he died that he always reported to Ike at the beginning and end of each working day, by phone or in person, and that it was "a very rare event" when he made a decision without Ike's consent, beforehand or subsequently. Ike exercised similar tight control over the Treasury, and strove mightily to reach a balanced budget each year, though he succeeded in doing so only twice in eight years. Still, this was a considerable achievement. Ike used to joke that his aim was to emulate President Jackson, and reduce the national debt to zero, but he added, "As Jackson was a Democrat, there must have been something fishy about it."

Ike recorded in his diary: "No one should be appointed to political office if he is a seeker after it." He also wrote: "We can afford to have only those people in high political offices who can afford to take them." Ideally, he wanted successful businessmen who made real financial sacrifices to take office, and men who had made their own way rather than inherited wealth and position. He appointed L. Sherman Adams, whom he knew a little, his chief assistant, then used him and Attorney General Herbert Brownell Jr. to sort through and vet the others. These included Joseph M. Dodge, director of the Bureau of the Budget, and Henry Cabot Lodge Jr., ambassador to the UN and another cabinet member. The defense secretary, Charles E. Wilson, president of General Motors, then the largest business in America, and the treasury secretary, George M. Humphrey, chairman of M. A. Hanna and Company, a large Ohio corporation, were thoroughly vetted but quite unknown to Ike. On his first meeting with Humphrey, Ike said: "Well, George, I see you part your hair the same way that I do." (Both were bald.) Douglas J. McKay, secretary of the interior, and Ezra Taft Benson, secretary of agriculture, were slight acquaintances, and the postmaster general (then a cabinet post), Arthur E. Summerfield, was known to him only as chairman of the Republican National Committee. As labor secretary Ike picked a Democrat, Martin P. Durkin of the American Federation of Labor's Plumbers and Steamfitters Union. The *New Republic* sneered: "Ike has picked a Cabinet of eight millionaires and one plumber." Actually, he also picked what he called "a statutory woman," Oveta Culp Hobby, whom he appointed to the "soft job" of Health, Education and Welfare. Ike had known her as a first-class head of the Women's Army Corps, and later as a prominent member of "Democrats for Ike." But she, as owner of a Texas newspaper, was a millionaire too.

The cabinet had no real power under Ike, as under most presidents, but he liked to consult them and get their views on domestic issues about which he knew or cared little. It was a strong and independent-minded body, and lasted well. Ike got to be fond of them, especially Humphrey, and financial policy — tight budget control, low or zero inflation, a strong dollar and minimum borrowing — was one of the big successes of the Eisenhower decade.

Ike regarded Dulles, the only one of his cabinet he knew at all well, as the prize member of his administration. "He has been in training for this job all his life," he said. "There is only one man I know who has seen *more* of the world, and talks with more people, and actually *knows* more than he does, and that's me," said Ike, "so we will make the most successful team in history." This was joking, of course, for Ike never boasted. But it was more or less true. Ike used Dulles very cleverly to give a hard edge to policy when required, and then applied his own emollient mixture to wrap up things. Oddly enough, however, Dulles had little to do with the most important success of the administration, the de facto peace armistice in Korea. Ike was criticized by the Democrats for saying, during the campaign, that he would go to Korea and make peace. This was "playing with the lives of Americans to get votes." He duly went to Korea, spent three days there and came back with the elements of what turned out to be the longest truce in history. It was all Ike's doing and the most popular act of his entire administration. It also saved the United States countless billions and made possible low or balanced budgets.

Ike said he "muttered a heartfelt

prayer" when the Korean truce went into operation. It is a curious fact that Ike, despite the religion of his parents, had never belonged to a religious community or gone to church regularly. Yet he introduced an element of religion into his presidency because he thought it ought to be there. He joined the Washington National Presbyterian Church and attended services regularly on Sundays. He wanted to set a good example. His view of religion was military — church parade, in effect. He said: "I believe there must be a spiritual force in American life, and in each person's life. And I don't care what it is." On inauguration day he took ten minutes to write a prayer to insert in his address. It made the speech what Lyndon Baines Johnson ironically called "a very good statement of Democratic progress in the last twenty years."

Ike found his job as president absorbing and fulfilling. The word he used was "exhilarating." It was the most open in American history in that exceptional facilities were provided for the press. He was the first to have a full-time press secretary, James C. "Jim" Hagerty, who set up a press conference every week, as well as for special events. At the end of his eight years in the White House, Ike had met the press on 193 occasions. From 1955, TV was invariably present. Ike was a brilliant performer and the media loved him. But it was a performance in more ways than one. Ike consistently misled the press not so much on specific matters but in giving a general impression that he worked much less than he did. He felt that if he made reporters believe he spent as much time as possible on the golf course, they would not push him too hard on particular issues and would let him get away with vagueness. Hagerty was instructed accordingly. In particular, he avoided giving any details of Ike's work before ten a.m., thus omitting the four busiest hours of Ike's day, in which his most important long-distance phone calls were made. I suspect that some of this deception was done for its own sake: Ike rather liked to display a twin persona: relaxed and easygoing, and ferociously hardworking. If he was not sure what the answers to expected questions were, he instructed Hagerty to speak gobbledygook, and Ike spoke it himself. He enjoyed the deliberate mangling of syntax and got a particular relish from clever imitations of his inarticulate use of English. Hagerty enjoyed the deception procedure — almost as elaborate, and successful, as the one used on German generals before D-Day. But Hagerty sometimes felt uneasy about misleading the press and feared he might be misled himself (he was). As Nixon grasped early on, Ike took to deviousness with relish.

Ike's White House was thus a place of smoke and mirrors. This extended to Mamie's domain. She would not have any details given of her own timetables when in the White House. The reason was that she liked to get up late and do a lot of work before she rose (like Churchill). She often remained in her room till ten a.m., or noon or even later. But she did not want this known. But she sometimes said: "Every woman over fifty should stay in bed till noon." She sometimes stayed in bed all day, especially on Sundays. She and Ike took every meal together when they were alone, and often her mother,

Mrs. Doud, ate with them. Mamie said: "I have only one career and his name is Ike." But she would not play golf or bridge with him because he yelled at her when she made mistakes. They were, however, a loving couple, especially in the White House. She said: "He needs me to be there. I need him for reassurance. I like it, during the night, when I stretch out my hand and feel his funny old bald head."

Ike did his best to generate a happy atmosphere both in the private part and in the public offices of the White House. He had an almost exaggerated wish to make everyone happy. He liked to bring as many people as was practicable into discussions, and generate a consensus. If possible, he heard all sides. Ike was happiest when everybody had been heard and everyone had agreed to what was finally decided. If that took place, he positively radiated contentment. Of course this wasn't always possible. After Julius and Ethel Rosenberg were convicted and sentenced for conspiracy to commit espionage, Ike refused to intervene in their execution. He said: "They have received the benefit of every safeguard which American justice can provide." The law must take its course. Ike was not worried — he thought justice had been done, and he lost no sleep over it.

McCarthyism was another matter. Some people felt at the time, and since, that Ike mishandled this issue. I suspect that any president would have done so, in one way or another. McCarthy was a uniquely unpleasant person, a phenomenon of a kind that — fortunately, rarely — appears in American life and flourishes mightily for a short time. Ike was sure it would not last long and that McCarthy would destroy himself, as indeed he did. Ike believed that anything he did, by giving him more publicity, would make things worse. He believed it called for the exercise of what, at times, is the most difficult of virtues: patience. He exercised patience, often against an angry chorus of well-meaning but excitable voices demanding action, and in the end he was proved right. He handed out the rope, and McCarthy hanged himself. Ike knew this would happen once the senator attacked the army. It exposed him to question by legal counsel, on TV, and showed a side of him the public had not seen before: McCarthy under pressure, and palpably lying. The public did not like what it saw. Ike was also able to outfox the senator by successfully pleading executive privilege in withholding information. McCarthy had always been a heavy drinker. He boasted of being able to "belt a fifth" (drink a fifth of a gallon of whiskey at a session). Now his intake increased rapidly. The end was pitiful. On December 2, 1954, after McCarthy's disastrous performance on TV during the army hearings, the Senate voted to "condemn" him by 67 to 22. Ike told the cabinet "the movement can now be called 'McCarthyism.' " He cut him from the list of dignitaries admitted to White House parties. Ike told his administration to boycott him. When McCarthy tried to take a place next to Nixon at a meeting in Milwaukee during the 1956 campaign (he was still a senator), an aide told him to leave. A reporter found him weeping. On May 2, 1957, he died of a diseased liver.

It was characteristic of Ike that he was rich in the unheroic virtues, such as patience. Nothing showed this more notably than his handling of the McCarthy issue, though it brought him at the time accusations of ignoble behavior. But it could be said in general that his whole approach to the cold war, in all its manifestations, was an exercise in patience. His aim was at all times to lower tension, never to raise it. He put his line of reasoning quite bluntly. "Military spending is far too high. Hell, this is peacetime! If you allow tension to rise, you increase the pressure to spend. If you lower it, the pressure eases, and you can make cuts." Ever since he had been in charge of the Philippines arms budget in the 1930s, he had felt passionately about the cost of armaments. Unusual in a professional soldier, his instincts were all in favor of economy. That is, once the needs of national security were satisfied, he grudged every dollar spent. This — it is an important point — reflected his training and experience as a staff general, as opposed to a fighting general. Staff generals were, or ought to be, concerned with the ability of the country to sustain military expenditure, as contrasted with simply demanding it. Now, as president, Ike was keenly aware, in addition, of what could be bought in civilian needs with any money saved on weapons.

Ike particularly disliked army, navy and air force chiefs engaging in sales pitches before Congress, especially in competition with one another and, most of all, as now happened increasingly, on TV. "They should keep their mouths shut" was his constant refrain. A lot of what they claimed, he said, was bunk. The current phrase on their lips, "the year of maximum danger," was bunk. He cut the defense budget Truman handed on to him by $10 billion. The United States, he said, must work harder to establish "reliance on allies." Quite early in his first term he delivered his "Chance for Peace" speech to the American Society of Newspaper Editors, in which he stressed the sheer financial and social cost of the cold war. He said: "We pay for a single fighter plane with a half million bushels of wheat. We pay for a single destroyer with new homes that could have housed more than 8,000 people." He declared: "This world in arms is not spending money alone. It is spending the sweat of its laborers, the genius of its scientists, the hopes of its children." These were amazing words coming from a general. To ram the point home, Ike put in an unusual (for him) poetic image: "Under the cloud of threatening war, it is humanity hanging from a cross of iron." There was an overwhelmingly favorable response to this striking speech.

Never absent from Ike's thoughts was the horror of nuclear weapons, and the risk of their use. When he became president, the United

States already had an armory of 1,600, and was adding to them at the rate of one a day. Unlike Truman (and later Kennedy and Johnson), Ike never seriously considered using one. On six separate occasions during his eight years in office, he decisively dismissed advice that they be deployed. But he was quite forthright in considering them part of the diplomatic and military game of chess he was playing with the Soviet Union. He had no qualms about positioning nuclear weapons on the periphery of Russia: by the mid-1950s, 36 percent of U.S. H-bombs and 42 percent of A-bombs were kept overseas. He authorized Lewis L. Strauss, chairman of the Atomic

Energy Commission (AEC), to test enormous multimegaton H-bombs: "Bravo! The biggest bomb the US ever detonated." He made an "Atoms for Peace" negotiating proposal at the UN in December 1953 and was disappointed the Russians did not respond. But he was not surprised. He was under no illusions about the difficulties of getting rid of the nuclear element in the cold war. He had no sympathy with J. Robert Oppenheimer, the "father of the A-bomb" and chairman of an advisory committee to the AEC, and agreed to the removal of his security clearance for "defects of character" (as opposed to actual disloyalty).

Ike was never a soft touch. He

was quite prepared to use deception, skullduggery and dirty tricks in advancing Western interests while avoiding bloodshed. He fully approved the CIA scheme to remove the Mohammad Mossadegh regime in Iran and restore the shah in August 1953. Operation Ajax, as it was called, was personally approved and ordered by Ike, who told Kermit "Kim" Roosevelt Jr., in charge of it, "Do it and don't bother me with the details." It was all top secret, and afterward Ike awarded Roosevelt the National Security Medal, again in secret.

He likewise eliminated the dangerous regime of President Jacobo Arbenz Guzmán in Guatemala, having satisfied himself it was a serious threat to American security that could not be met by other means. It was decided with Allen W. Dulles, head of the CIA, at a Sunday brunch. The scheme was modeled on Ajax and took place in June 1954. At his first press conference to be broadcast, on January 19, 1955, Ike said ending the Arbenz threat was one of his proudest successes, and it is the only covert CIA job he mentions in his memoirs.

On entering office, Ike had written down, on a scrap of paper and under the heading "The Big Issues," the following: taxes, budget, Korea, defense spending, foreign aid and world peace. By July 26, 1953, he had succeeded, despite opposition from Syngman Rhee, John Foster Dulles and Republican diehards, in ending the fighting in Korea, which had reached a stalemate but was costing a thousand American casualties a week. This was, as it seemed at the time, one of Ike's greatest achievements, and he compounded it by diverting a large part of the money saved to building up the South Korean economy, thus laying the foundations of what was to become one of the strongest economies in Asia. Equally important, certainly in retrospect, was his decision to stay out of Vietnam, and if his successors had stuck to his guidance, history would have been different, and happier. He wanted people to say of his presidency: "He got us out of Korea, and he kept us out of Vietnam." Ike believed many mistakes had been made because Americans had insisted on overruling local leaders. "The reason we lost China," Ike said, "was because Marshall insisted Chiang Kai-shek take Communists into his government, against Chiang's judgment."

Ike had supported NATO from its inception, and he always believed the United States should maintain a military commitment to Europe. But he thought the European powers should make a contribution to their own defense commensurate with their resources, and that it should be entirely under their own control as far as possible.

That is why he welcomed the proposal for the European Defense
Community (EDC) or "European
Army," originally a French idea, as
an alternative to rearming Germany. But the French National Assembly rejected the EDC. Ike,
pragmatic as always, did not repine
but responded by bringing Germany into NATO. "Long faces
don't win wars, or avoid them" was
a saying of his. The scheme he supported was for Germany to have an
army limited to twelve divisions,
without nuclear weapons, under
NATO command. "Better than the
EDC," he eventually decided. This
was approved by the French National Assembly by a vote of 319–
264, regarded rightly as a triumph

for Ike, and duly ratified by Congress.

Ike was not too upset when the midterm elections deprived the Republicans of a majority (they lost eighteen seats in the House and two in the Senate) because he had always been sure that sensible government demanded a progressive Republican Party throughout the country. Failing this, he knew he could get by on all key foreign policy and defense issues with a coalition of liberal Republicans and Eisenhower Democrats, particularly in the South. That meant, as he privately recognized, that he would have to run again. He enjoyed being president, on the whole. When General Montgomery, visiting him at Augusta, asked what it was like, he replied: "It's pound, pound, pound. Not only is your intellectual capacity taxed to the utmost, but so is your physical stamina." But he said this with a grin. He received Churchill as a guest too, but found that he was too old to do serious business. Ike recorded in his diary his dismay at the folly of many of those on his side of the political spectrum. He found the Republican senator William F. "Bill" Knowland "one of the most stupid men in the United States." He noted of the American Medical Association, "Daily I am impressed by the shortsightedness bordering on tragic stupidity of many who fancy themselves to be the greatest believers in a system of carefulness." He did his best to bring forward men of talent by a series of stag dinners, attended by the most powerful men in America. These were very successful. Ike always spoke last, and the keynote was gentle persuasion. Ambassador (to the Soviet Union) George F. Kennan commented on one of them: "In summarizing the group's conclusions, President Eisenhower showed his intellectual ascendancy over every man in the room."

He never lost sight of the need to lower tension. One of his favorite quotes was from General Robert E. Lee: "It is well that war is so terrible. Were it not so, we would grow too fond of it." He said it was good for him to be obliged to write letters of condolence to the next of kin of U.S. servicemen who died on duty. It was "a very sobering experience." He told reporters at a press conference: "Don't go to war in response to emotions of anger and resentment. Do it prayerfully."

One of Ike's strategies was to confuse both his opponents and, on occasion, his supporters. This, for instance, was the aim of the so-called Formosa doctrine. It was his idea, and it authorized Ike to "use force" if he detected a threat to the United States in the Formosa area. Congress in effect gave the president a blank check. In January 1955, the House approved it 410 to 3, the Senate 83 to 3. The aim was to puzzle the Chinese and Russians. He said to Hagerty: "Don't worry, Jim. If that question comes up I'll just confuse them." It was one of the occasions when Ike used garbled syntax. Ike did not honestly know whether China would attack Quemoy and Matsu. He thought not. "But then things are often unsure," he said. "Deliberate ambiguity and deception" were the key. He wanted as many options as possible all the time, and he got them. His handling of the "Q and M crisis" was, in retrospect, one of the triumphs of his career. The penalty for miscalculation was underlined by Operation Alert, a simulated H-bomb attack on the United States involving national martial law and casualties of 150 million. This was a prelude to Ike's Open Skies proposal, which he presented at the summit meeting held in July 1955 in Geneva. It achieved nothing but goodwill but, as Ike said, "Good will is always worth having, and it's certainly better than bad will."

On September 23, 1955 having performed with credit at the summit, Ike had a heart attack (coronary thrombosis) while on holiday near Denver. He was taken to Fitzsimons Army Hospital. It was a serious business but never critical, and Ike was in control virtually throughout. His instructions to Hagerty were adamant: "Tell the truth. The whole truth.

Don't try to conceal anything."
Hagerty knew exactly how to
handle things, and the inurbanity
of his bulletins served cleverly to
divert attention from difficult questions. One began: "The big news
today is that the President had a
successful bowel movement this
morning." Congress was not in session, fortunately, and though Ike
was in the hospital for six weeks —
during which he informed himself
thoroughly on the position of army
nurses, and wrote an acute and
useful letter on their problems —
he was able to carry on work after
the first few days, receiving sixty-
six official visitors. Ike recovered
remarkably quickly and was able to
return to Washington, D.C., on

November 11, then recuperated at Gettysburg. The house now had a glassed-in porch that caught the sun beautifully and a putting green that Ike put to constant use. Mamie was delighted with the house and robustly unfazed by the heart attack. The farm now had an Angus herd that gave Ike endless pleasure. Should Ike run again? She was definite: "I just can't believe Ike's work is finished," she ruled. General Howard M. Snyder, Ike's personal physician, thought his life expectancy would improve if he ran for a second term. Ike was influenced chiefly by the poor quality of the alternatives: "Nincompoops!" He thought Harriman "nothing but a Park Avenue Truman." He added:

"I just hate to turn the country back into the hands of people like Stevenson, Harriman, and Kefauver." The people he liked were Brownell, Adams, Anderson and Humphrey, but none of them had much chance of nomination.

Ike's decision to run was influenced by the fact that he had been obliged on a number of occasions (five or by some counts six) to reject flatly official advice to use nuclear weapons against China. With his military background and prestige he could do so with impunity. But others? He told Hagerty: "My one purpose is to keep the world at peace." At a big secret dinner on January 15, 1956, his closest advisers were unanimous in favor of a second term. He told them he got to sleep easily but woke early. "But then I always have. I'm sixty-five. There are times when I feel I have never been happier." By February 12, he had decided to run again, and on TV he said he could perform all the duties. He saved a great deal of agitation by taking only a limited interest in domestic issues, believing time and prosperity would cure most problems, including civil rights. He cared about the soil bank, and he put through the greatest interstate highway program in American history. This was his memorial. His decision to run again survived an attack of ileitis on June 8, 1956. This onset was very severe.

He was rushed to Walter Reed Hospital and the next day underwent surgery. But the operation was successful and his recovery rapid. On August 23, the Republican National Convention gave Ike the nomination by acclamation.

The international scene in the second half of 1956 was dominated by the so-called Suez crisis. The year before, Churchill had retired and, against his better judgment and Ike's, had handed over the reins to Sir Anthony Eden, whom Ike knew to be a sick man. Eden tried to push ahead with the Baghdad Pact, a device that was modeled on SEATO (Southeast Asia Treaty Organization) but was, in reality, an attempt to shore up

Britain's waning power in the Middle East. Ike was not interested — the area and its frantic Arab politicians irritated and bored him — and he considered the plan of the Egyptian dictator, Colonel Gamal Abdel Nasser, to build a new high dam on the Nile misconceived and vainglorious. So he withdrew American financial support, obliging Britain to do the same. In retaliation, Nasser seized the Suez Canal, owned and run by an Anglo-French company.

Eden regarded this act as a threat to vital British interests, and eventually decided to meet it by devising a secret plan in conjunction with the French and Israelis. Under this agreement, Israel would invade

Egypt and occupy the canal. Britain and France would then send in troops "to separate the combatants." Eden never cleared this bizarre plan with Ike — his one hope of its succeeding — and Ike first learned of it with surprise and consternation, indeed anger. The Middle East occupied very little of his time. The diaries of Ann Whitman, his confidential secretary, give a good idea of what occupied his mind. He spent between twenty and thirty hours on each major speech, and often spotted mistakes everyone else had missed. He was a perfectionist, and really better at working up a subject than any of those supposed to help him. Charles Wilson, the defense secretary, took up more of Ike's time than any other cabinet officer because of interservice rivalry, which Ike detested. Had it not been for these conflicts, Ike might have had a better grasp of the Middle East. As it was, he left it to Dulles, who was obtuse and who found Eden insufferable (a feeling that was mutual). General Andrew J. Goodpaster gave Ike a half hour's intelligence briefing most mornings, but it usually dealt with Russian and Chinese intentions.

The climax of the Anglo-French-Israeli collusive plan in Egypt, unfortunately, coincided with the climax of Ike's reelection campaign. He decided that the plan, which he viewed with a mixture of moral outrage, professional military contempt and diplomatic distaste, could not be allowed to succeed. He raged: "I've never seen great powers make such a *mess* and *botch* of things." In a later exchange of letters with Churchill, he complained that "even by the doctrine of expediency, the invasion of Egypt could not be judged as soundly conceived and skillfully executed." At the United Nations, Ike took the line that the United States must support "the victim of aggression" (that is, Egypt) and at the same time he privately told George Humphrey that the U.S. Treasury should be "unhelpful" to Britain, whose currency was coming under pressure as a result of Eden's folly.

The run on sterling eventually did the trick of forcing Eden to climb down and, shortly afterward, resign. Ike found the whole business repellent: "There's no people I'd rather fight alongside than the British. But this thing — my God!" At the same time, "if the Soviets attack the French and British we would be justified in taking military action even if Congress is not in session."

Ike, as he had warned his supporters, limited his campaign for reelection to three or four big speeches, mainly on TV. Keeping the peace was the issue. Privately he thought "Stevenson and Kefauver, as a combination, are the sorriest and weakest pair that ever aspired to the highest office in the land." Stevenson's call for a ban on atomic tests — promptly echoed by the Soviet leader Nikolai Bulganin — enraged Ike. He told Dulles to publish a document on the ban "so factual as to be uninteresting," a good example of the obfuscation that Ike found so useful at times. He left the routine campaigning to Nixon, who responded obediently, as he always did.

Ike's attitude toward Nixon remains a mystery to this day. He behaved toward his vice president throughout the eight years they served together as if he were a burden or an embarrassment rather than an asset. Asked if Nixon had ever made a positive contribution to his administration, Ike avoided an answer and said he'd like to think about it. Of course Ike had never actually chosen Nixon to run with him. And he disliked having around him a man he could not fire.

The campaign was lackluster and the result a foregone conclusion. It remains unclear why the Democrats chose Stevenson to run a second time. Probably they regarded Ike as unbeatable by anyone they had on offer, and Stevenson was a dignified and honorable loser. Ike compared himself during the campaign to Admiral Horatio Nelson, who famously asked about the enemy ships "Are there any of them left?" He was furious with Stevenson for not conceding sooner: "What in the name of God is the monkey waiting for?" Stevenson carried only seven states, and Ike's plurality of 10 million votes — 35,581,003 to 25,738,763 — was far greater than the 1952 majority. But Ike failed to recover Congress. He did not repine. His strategy of cultivating southern Democrats in key votes served well throughout his second term on issues he cared about. Ike summed up: "America is a rich country. Provided we can avoid war, keep tension low, and avoid absurdly high defense budgets, we will prosper, sure enough."

■ ■ ■ ■

PART SEVEN:
THE BEST
DECADE IN
AMERICAN
HISTORY

■ ■ ■ ■

The Suez crisis, and Ike's response to it, had the inadvertent effect of making the United States the hero of the third world. At the UN, Ike tabled what was, in effect, a pro-Egyptian motion, which brought "tremendous acclaim" from small nations. The UN secretary-general, Dag Hammarskjöld, called it "one of the great moments in UN history." Ike found himself popular in quarters that usually regarded him with suspicion, if not hostility. He noted: "The United States now enjoys a reputation it has not held since the end of World War Two." After Harold Macmillan replaced Eden in London, the breach with Britain was soon healed. Sir Harold Caccia, the British ambassador in Washington, D.C., and Winthrop Aldrich, the pro-British ambassador in London, worked hard to rebuild "the special relationship." Ike said: "We furnished a lot of fig-leaves."

For a time he found the unusual applause of the third world delightful, and encouraged it. He made the so-called Eisenhower doctrine, of friendliness toward the Arab states and benevolence in the Middle East, the theme of his second inaugural. To reproachful letters from Freddie de Guingand, General Hastings Ismay and Air Marshal Arthur Tedder, he replied that the United States had to "preserve a place that is correct and moral."

Ike personally presented to Congress an aspect of his Middle Eastern "doctrine" which allowed him to make military interventions in the area on his own judgment. This caused no trouble. But he could not get his foreign aid bill passed: it was cut down from $4 billion to $2.76 billion and, therefore, "emasculated." He did his best to suck up to Arab or Middle Eastern potentates such as Habib Bourguiba of Tunisia. He was cordial to Pandit Nehru of India, who was eager to act as broker between East and West, particularly in the Arab world. Dulles was particularly keen that Ike should be gracious to King Saud of Saudi Arabia. Robert Wagner, the mayor of New York, refused to meet him at the airport, saying "he is not the kind of person we want to officially recognize in New York City." His flight was switched to Washington, D.C., with King Saud hinting he would not come at all unless the president met him at the airport. Ike told Dulles: "Of course I will meet him. My worry is that he will bring his harem." The meeting duly took place, the talk ranging over shooting rifles and the king's preference for using hawks.

Ike complained he was "almost suf-focated by the musky odor coming from the robes of the monarch and his suite." The king, however, did not bring his harem. The problem, said Ike, was "gratuities." He had imposed a nontipping rule at the White House, and the king spread $50 and $100 notes like confetti, which Ike had somehow to gather up and render harmless.

Mamie kept out of the king's way. But she was always a powerful pres-ence in the White House. Ike gave her high marks throughout his tenure. She was cheerful, well groomed, perfectly dressed in her deliberately unadventurous fashion. She supervised entertainment on a huge scale, and made sure each member of the large staff got suitable Christmas and birthday presents. But she avoided talk about professional presidential matters unless Ike deliberately consulted her, which was rare. He was not interested in women except in a domestic setting. He sent Clare Boothe Luce to Italy as ambassador and appointed women to twenty-eight positions sufficiently senior to require Senate confirmation. But when the Equal Rights Amendment came up at press conferences, he tended to turn questions into a joke: "It's hard for a mere man to believe that a woman doesn't have equal rights!" But he admitted: "I just probably haven't been active enough in doing something about it!"

Nothing much came of Ike's idea of becoming the champion of the third world and befriending small powers. The smaller players on the world chessboard tend, like the big ones, to follow their own best interests, and gratitude is not a factor. The United States, too, followed its interests. On July 14, 1958, a military coup in Iraq destroyed Nuri Said, the pro-British strongman, the ruling family and most of the political establishment. The following day, at the request of President Camille Chamoun of Lebanon, Ike agreed to send troops there as a precautionary move. Two days later, in a completely separate movement, British paratroops landed in Jordan at the request of King Hussein. The following phone conversation took place between Ike and Macmillan. Ike: "We are going into Beirut. Chamoun wants us." Macmillan: "You are doing a Suez on me, ha ha!" Ike: "The Jordanians want us, too, but you must do it — do a Suez on me, ha ha!" Macmillan: "Mum's the word."

These separate but not wholly uncoordinated twin operations were the most successful of their kind in the whole of the cold war. The damage in Iraq had already been done, and could not be remedied. But U.S.-British troop movements limited the erosion to a minimum. There was no fighting, and there were no casualties in either operation, and in both cases the troops were withdrawn by November. This was the only American military operation abroad that Ike initiated in the whole of his eight years at the White House, and it was completely successful. It was no accident, because Ike, in addition to his presidential authority, was a very experienced and successful general who knew exactly what troops could, and could not, do. The contrast between Ike's movement into Lebanon and John F. Kennedy's abortive Bay of Pigs misadventure in the next presidency — leading directly to the Cuban missile crisis, when the USSR and the United States came

close to thermonuclear war —
could not have been more marked.
In international affairs, especially
in their military aspects, Ike's touch
was always sure. The cold war
inevitably had its dangers, but
insofar as they could be reduced to
a minimum, Ike contrived to do so.

Not that Ike was ever careless of
America's security. Quite the contrary. He was always careful to
ensure a wide margin of superiority for the United States over the
USSR both in strategic weapons
and in conventional forces in areas
he deemed vital. To the stockpile of
1,500 nuclear weapons he inherited, he continued to add at the
rate of 2 a day, so that by 1959
there were more than 6,000. The

figures were given to Ike orally by the head of the Atomic Energy Commission, and Ike not only was well informed about the composition and deployment of the stockpile but frequently issued orders for changes in response to developing technology. The Russians were making nuclear weapons at what seemed a frantic rate throughout the Eisenhower presidency. Many of them had a huge megatonnage. But Ike was satisfied that the disposition of U.S. weapons — the means of delivery, the early warning systems in use and the timings — gave America a decisive advantage in the nuclear field. He also ensured that reliable U.S. allies had nuclear forces that were up to date and adequate, for instance through the provision of technology enabling Britain to equip her Polaris-type submarines with long-distance nuclear missiles. This agreement Ike negotiated personally with Harold Macmillan, and it was so well judged that it is still, in essence, in force more than half a century later.

On October 4, 1957, came the surprising news of the launch of the Soviet *Sputnik.* To what extent this was a shock to Ike is unclear. He was fully aware of the enormous effort the USSR was making in rocket technology. From the start of his presidency, he had authorized close surveillance of Soviet rocket sites. He had approved the design and production of the U-2 high-altitude surveillance aircraft, of which thirty were made on his instructions, and he ordered its use as soon as it had been successfully tested. Ike never had any qualms about such weapons because he regarded them as essential to military intelligence gathering, even if, strictly speaking, they involved violating international law. It is true he wanted to keep the U-2 secret as long as possible, and he had been assured by Allen Dulles, head of the CIA, that no U-2 pilot would fall into the hands of the Russians. This proved to be untrue. On May 1, 1960, a U-2 was shot down over the Urals by a new long-range Russian antiaircraft missile. The pilot,

Francis Gary Powers, had been issued a suicide pill, but he was also provided with a parachute and he used it. Ike's comments on the business were guarded and circumspect. Not so the carefully prepared fury of Nikita Khrushchev, the Soviet leader. The U-2 flight was given as the reason for the failure of the summit held in Paris on May 16–19, 1960. But the meeting, which involved Macmillan and de Gaulle, as well as the American and Russian leaders, had been over-hyped, and would have proved a disappointment in any case. Khrushchev's excitable behavior, in taking advantage of Ike's presumed discomfiture, was crude and unimpressive. On this, and on other occasions, even at the UN, he took off his shoe and banged it on the speaker's rostrum. This was part of an ascending curve of clownish activity that marked his time as sole director of Soviet affairs, which climaxed in the Cuban missile crisis, and it formed part of the dossier used against him when his colleagues on the Soviet presidium, in October 1964, decided to get rid of him. By contrast, Ike kept his cool, and his self-possession. The summit came in the middle of a program of foreign visits that marked the closing years of Ike's presidency. They were marked by the enthusiasm with which he was received everywhere and the perception of him as a "man of peace" with a reputation for reducing tension and seeking negotiated ways out of potential war situations.

Nevertheless, in its day and for long after, the Russian launching of *Sputnik* gave Ike problems. It came as a profound shock to the American public and reversed a growing mood of complacency about the cold war and the arms race. The media, or the less well-informed sections of it, proclaimed that America had lost its technological lead and forfeited the space race. Something akin to a national crisis of self-confidence developed. And in the midst of this, Ike, on November 25, 1957, had a stroke. For a few moments he could not talk. Ann Whitman was a witness.

This was Ike's third serious illness in less than two years, when he was sixty-seven years old. Nevertheless, he was determined to stay and to take up his full duties as soon as possible. He did so, indeed. But it was noticeable that he was more irritable and short-tempered than before. He noticed it himself. In fact, he said that from the Suez business onward, his life had been a succession of crises. He also wrote: "The year 1958 was the worst year of my life."

That was because he was working, in effect, with a new team. In the autumn of 1957, some of the cabinet strongmen, who had insisted all along that they would serve only for a limited time, decided to go. Humphrey left the Treasury on July 29; Charlie Wilson resigned from Defense on October 8; Brownell gave up as attorney general on November 8. Ike missed them. All had their weaknesses, but they, plus John Foster Dulles, of course, did most of the talking at cabinet meetings, including arguing with Ike. It was "the break-up of a team," as Ike put it, and for him, team and team spirit provided the essence of a good administration. Dulles remained but was visibly failing. Ike had the highest opinion of him, as we have seen, but he noted that he had no friends in the public sphere, being regarded as "legalistic, arrogant, sanctimonious, and arbitrary." The fact is, Ike made the decisions, and if they were unpopular (as many were), Dulles took the blame. But the public did not know the extent to which Ike was absolutely in charge, and Dulles a mere executant. Dulles, at Ike's insistence, carried on as long as possible, but in April 1959 he was forced to resign, dying five weeks later. His successor, Christian Herter, had none of his authority or his value to Ike as a lightning rod. And Ike had already lost his personal assistant, Sherman Adams, a casualty of an uncharacteristic business relationship with the industrialist Bernard Goldfine. Adams was finally obliged to resign on September 22, 1958, on the eve of the midterm elections.

Adams's imprudence, however, was not the cause of the Republican disaster at midterm. It was a delayed reaction to the Soviet *Sputnik,* and the spin the Democratic political strategists succeeded in putting on it in the form of the so-called missile gap. This never actually existed, and was never precisely defined. But the public's imagination was captured by the notion of a catastrophic "gap" between America and the Soviet Union in missile capability and delivery systems. Satisfied there was no gap, Ike declined to address himself to the problem, which he saw as entirely political.

As a result of the popular perception, Ike's party went down to defeat. The Democrats now controlled the Senate by 64 to 34, and the House by 283 to 153. More serious in some ways was the Democratic hegemony in the state capitols. They now had thirty-five governors, the Republicans only fourteen. Some commentators regarded it as the party's worst defeat since the Great Depression. Ike recorded that he now had the "dubious distinction" of being the first president to face three successive opposition Congresses. Ike himself, however, remained hugely popular and could usually get what he wanted by using southern Democrats. Ann Whitman, "that most devoted friend and slave," as he called her, recorded in her diary, "things have been hellish" but "I never cease to admire more and more the attitude of this man under pressure."

Indeed, Ike's characterization of 1958 as "the worst year of my life" was a shade ironic. He recorded in his notes that he was "fine" and "felt younger." Throughout his second term he was bothered and sometimes baffled by the civil rights problem. This was not an issue on which he had strong views or a definite program. Ike was not color conscious. He was not exactly color-blind either. He tended to take the view that acute color problems usually grew out of wide disparities of wealth, and that rising prosperity would reduce them to a tolerable level. His job, as president, was to keep the wealth flowing, to ensure that it was widely distributed and that Americans saw the system as, broadly speaking, "fair." It was a word he often used, with approval. He liked to say: "We live in a fair society." The second point he always stressed was the duty of everyone to obey the law, in all circumstances.

Ike came up against the demands of both fairness and the need to obey the law in the late summer of 1957, in Little Rock, Arkansas. The governor, Orval Faubus, defied a federal court order desegregating the Central High School, and ordered in the Arkansas National

Guard in support of his action. Ike had earlier ruled out such a situation as impossible, and when it happened, he at first tried to avoid confrontation. Over the Little Rock crisis, he and Herbert Brownell, the attorney general, had so many conversations on the phone that Ann Whitman's superb monitoring system, which had hitherto survived all the emergencies of the cold war, could not cope. Ike's way of dealing with this kind of crisis was to deny it existed, and that usually worked. But in the Little Rock case, he was reluctantly obliged to send in federal troops — elements of the 101st Airborne Division — and to remove the local national guard from Faubus's command

and put it under federal control. The soldiers went in on September 25, and were in Little Rock till the end of November. Ike always hated using troops for tasks outside their professional duties, whether for cold war intervention or to contain civilian conflict. As with the Lebanon crisis, he pulled out the troops as early as possible, and to judge by the ferocity with which he was assailed both by southern whites and by civil rights leaders, he probably acted wisely both in sending troops and in removing them. But he regarded the entire business with distaste and had no zest in speaking about it. He noted it was the first time since Reconstruction that federal troops had been dispatched to the South to protect the rights of blacks. Sherman Adams recorded that, to Ike, the action was "a constitutional duty which was the most repugnant to him of all his acts in his eight years at the White House."

Much more to his taste, and perfectly suited to his diplomatic and military skills, was the Berlin crisis that marked the final period of his presidency. In November 1958, Khrushchev escalated tensions over the city by insisting that unless American troops left Berlin by May 27, 1959, he would sign a treaty with the East German government providing the right to deny ground access to West Berlin. Ike handled this provocation, so typical of his confrontational and unpredictable opponent, in masterly style. He refused to raise the stakes by calling Khrushchev's bluff. He denied there was a crisis. He kept everyone talking. He flatly refused demands to increase spending to prepare for "another Berlin crisis." He told a group of Republican leaders who came to the White House, "I am getting awfully sick of the lobbying of the munitions. You begin to see this thing isn't wholly the defense of the country, but only more money for some who are already fat cats." In fact, Ike finessed the so-called crisis pretty well. He got through it without war, without backing down and without increasing the defense budget, and Berlin remained totally unchanged.

However, what Ike labeled "the lobbying of the munitions" stuck in his memory. It became the underlying theme of his last period. Ike felt that he was handing over the nation in reasonably good shape to his successors. Despite the antics of Khrushchev, a man he disliked and despised, tension was not high. There was no "missile gap." America was prosperous and solvent. Inflation was low. With considerable difficulty, he had kept defense spending under control; in two years he had balanced the budget; and in the remaining six, the deficits had been reasonable. Ike's personal standing had never been higher, and he knew he was respected all over the nation, and in some quarters loved.

Yet when Ike stepped down in January 1961, he was deeply worried. He had done his best to get Nixon elected even though he had grave reservations about his fitness to be president. But these were as nothing to his doubts about the winner, John F. Kennedy. He thought Kennedy "came of bad stock," was "reckless" and would "get America into bad trouble." These fears were linked to apprehensions about the country's future. He thought the United States was known in the world for its military strength rather than its uniqueness as a democratic haven of freedom. The military strength, and imprudent leadership, could lead the country into interventions all over the world, encouraged by the arms lobby and the military chiefs who were its puppets, and the result would be an overextension of resources and economic ruin.

This had been the theme, in private, of a number of meetings Ike had had with military and political intimates in his final years as president. But now, before stepping down, he decided to go public. His friends had been expecting that his farewell address, on January 17, 1961, would be sentimental and valedictory. But instead it was a serious warning. Ike decided his best, last service to the nation was to draw attention to the way in which even a rich country could undermine its economy by over-spending on armaments. His words were carefully chosen and striking and need to be quoted in full:

Until the latest of our world con-flicts, the United States had no armaments industry. American makers of plowshares could, with time and as required, make swords as well. But now we can no longer risk emergency improvi-sation of national defense; we have been compelled to create a permanent armaments industry of vast proportions. Added to this, three and a half million men and women are directly engaged in the defense establishment. We annually spend on military security more than the net income of all United States corporations.

This conjunction of an immense military establishment and a large arms industry is new in the American experience. The total influence — economic, political, even spiritual — is felt in every city, every State house, every office of the Federal government. We recognize the imperative need for this development. Yet we must not fail to comprehend its grave implications. Our toil, resources and livelihood are all involved; so is the very structure of our society.

In the councils of government, we must guard against the acquisition of unwarranted influence, whether sought or unsought, by the military-industrial complex. The potential for the disastrous rise of misplaced power exists and will persist.

We must never let the weight of this combination endanger our liberties or democratic processes.

Ike followed this up, the next day, with a press conference in which he made an impassioned attack on the way military values were replacing the bedrock civil values of American society. He said photos of Titan or Atlas missiles were found in every magazine, and he decried "a great influence, almost an insidious penetration of our own minds that the only thing this country is engaged in is weaponry and missiles. And I'll tell you we just can't afford to do that. The reason we have them is to protect the great values in which we believe, and they are far deeper even than our own lives and our own property, as I see it."

Ike said that someone had to defend the economy as a whole because "it is the nature of our government that everyone, except for a thin layer at the top, is working knowingly or unknowingly, to damage our economy, the reason being that they see the need for more and more resources for their own service or agency, and the valuable results that can be achieved through added effort in their own particular element." Against this, someone at the top had to ensure that the economy as a whole remained "viable and strong."

It cannot be said that Ike's successors heeded his warning. Ike had a low opinion of John F. Kennedy, his family and the kind of administration he formed. He was vastly amused by Harold Macmillan's verdict, after an early visit to the new regime: "The Kennedy occupation of Washington was like watching the Borgia brothers taking over a respectable north Italian town." That made Ike laugh, ruefully.

Still, he had given America a

decade of unexampled prosperity and calm. The country had emerged from the Korean War and the excesses of McCarthyism. Inflation was low. Budgets were in balance or with manageable deficits. The military-industrial complex was kept under control. Seen from the perspective of the twenty-first century, the Eisenhower years, 1953 to 1961, were the climax of "the American Century." The GNP rose (in constant 1958 dollars) from $355.3 billion in 1950 to $452.5 billion in 1957, an improvement of 27.4 percent or nearly 4 percent per year. By 1960, it had increased to $487.7 billion, or 37 percent for the 1950s as a whole. By 1960, the average family income was $5,620, 30 percent higher in real purchasing power than in 1950. By then, 62 percent of houses were owner occupied, compared with 43 percent in 1940 and 55 percent in 1950. Thanks to Ike's fiscal restraint, prices remained stable and unemployment only a little more than 4 percent.

This glorious decade reflected much longer-term and worldwide expansion of international trade and industrial production. Between 1705 and 1971, production rose no fewer than 1,736 times, most of it in the post-1948 quarter century, and especially in the United States, now by far the largest industrial economy. In the same quarter century, 1948–71, world trade rose at an annual average of 7.27 percent, at its highest rate during the Eisenhower years. Nothing like this had ever been experienced before. Nothing like it, except for brief episodes, has been experienced since. These statistics are worth recalling, because they help to explain why the 1950s are now seen as a golden age when American power and, still more, American prosperity acted as the parameters of a stable and peaceful world. Ike's warning that paying for the power could imperil the prosperity was not heeded, with results that he foresaw. And so the American Century passed, and the world moved on.

Ike ceased to be president on

January 20, 1961, and enjoyed eight years of retirement at his Gettysburg farm, hunting, fishing, playing golf and bridge, and talking with friends. He died, aged seventy-eight, on March 28, 1969, after a productive, successful and, on the whole, remarkably happy life. His last words (to his son) were: "I want to go. God take me."

FURTHER READING

J. Ronald Oakley, *God's Country: America in the Fifties* (New York: Dembner Books, 1986) is a good general survey, and an excellent personal account is Stephen Ambrose, *Eisenhower: Soldier and President* (New York: Simon and Schuster, 1990). I also recommend Michael Korda, *Ike: An American Hero* (New York: Harper, 2007); Jean Edward Smith, *Eisenhower in War and Peace* (New York: Random House, 2012); Evan Thomas, *Ike's Bluff: President Eisenhower's Secret Battle to Save the World* (New York: Little, Brown, 2012); Robert F. Burk, *Dwight D. Eisenhower: Hero and Politician* (Boston: Twayne, 1986); Craig Allen, *Eisenhower and the Mass Media: Peace, Prosperity, and Prime-Time TV* (Chapel Hill: University of North Carolina Press, 1993); William B. Pickett, *Eisenhower and American Power* (Wheeling, Ill.: Harlan Davidson, 1995); Fred I. Greenstein, *The Hidden Hand Presidency: Eisenhower as Leader* (New York: Basic Books, 1982); and Robert A. Divine, *Eisenhower and the Cold War* (New York: Oxford University Press, 1981).

ABOUT THE AUTHOR

Paul Johnson is the author of the bestselling biographies *Napoleon: A Penguin Life* and *Churchill,* among others. He writes a monthly column for *Forbes* and has also written for *The Wall Street Journal, The New York Times* and many other publications. He lives in London.